BEYOND THE MYTHS

THE JOURNEY TO ADULTHOOD

To Woody —
A solid colleague
in ministry —
Dan Bagby
6/28/2007

Smyth & Helwys Publishing, Inc.
6316 Peake Road
Macon, Georgia 31210-3960
1-800-747-3016
©2007 by Smyth & Helwys Publishing
All rights reserved.
Printed in the United States of America.

The paper used in this publication meets the minimum requirements of
American National Standard for Information Sciences—
Permanence of Paper for Printed Library Materials.
ANSI Z39.48–1984. (alk. paper)

Library of Congress Cataloging-in-Publication Data

Bagby, Daniel G.
Beyond the myths : the journey to adulthood / by Daniel Bagby.
p. cm.
ISBN 978-1-57312-488-1 (pbk. : alk. paper)
1. Youth—Conduct of life. 2. Adolescent psychology.
3. Youth—Religious life. 4. Pastoral psychology.
5. Pastoral counseling.
I. Title.

BJ1661.B27 2007
248.8'4—dc22

2007005457

Contents

Introduction

Never has the task of becoming an adult in our society been more challenging than now. The journey from late adolescence to young adulthood is paved with pitfalls and obstacles of significant proportions. Today's adolescents struggle with the complex issues of identity, sexuality, intimacy, vocation, purpose, and spirituality. They are on their own, yet still dependent; they are free to choose, while shackled by overwhelming choices. They are scrutinized and ignored, coddled and neglected, encouraged and demeaned, empowered and impaired.

Faced with such bewildering and distressing concerns, young people in our North American society are redesigning the first movements toward adulthood. Disguised as adults in a culture that has emotionally or developmentally ill equipped them for the tasks of adulthood, many people in their twenties—and early thirties—have sought a variety of ways to "buy" themselves time to work on the recipe of embracing the requirements of adulthood. Fearful of making long-term commitments and decisions on the basis of short-term insights, the "provisional adult" (as Gail Sheehy called them in *New Passages* [New York: Ballentine Books, 1996]) takes a job, goes to school, joins the military, or finds another form of temporary distraction while agonizing quietly with a restless discomfort over not feeling ready for the long-term commitments of adulthood.

These "tentative" adults also know that many "settled" older adults are neither settled nor as certain about themselves as they appear. The new adults have lived in families where marriages have collapsed, jobs have ended, dreams have dissolved, and vocational goals apparently have failed to deliver their promised fulfillment to prior generations. Wars and "rumors of wars" also appear to be a way of life rather than an unusual news item.

In such a time of troubled family stability, the local church seems poised either to play the role of a family of origin in which young adults can no longer function, or to assume a crucial supportive role as a steady family in bewildering days. The body of Christ—distracted itself by its own struggles with change and identity—has an opportunity and challenge today to provide an environment in which developing adults may safely navigate the perilous waters from late adolescence to full adulthood. Whether the church of the twenty-first century will offer assistance to beleaguered young adults—or become irrelevant in the conversation—remains to be seen. One thing is certain: important issues need to be identified and addressed in order to care for and sustain young adults transitioning from late adolescence to the experience of young adulthood.

What are the major issues defining and challenging young adults today? In what ways can we help young people sift through the confusion of messages they are hearing—to listen to whatever promptings are of benefit and value in this delicate journey of becoming? How can communities of faith and institutions of learning help—and not harm—young people pursuing pointers and purpose as they seek to "grow up"? The following pages are an attempt to identify some of the unique challenges confronting today's emerging young adult. They are also an attempt to distinguish between fact and fiction as adolescents "come of age." This exciting and fragile transition is one of self-discovery, self-scrutiny, and self-preoccupation, requiring discernment, patience, and wisdom; it should not have to be made alone.

The first pages of this study identify the unique struggles of today's young adults in regard to self-development (imagining, seeking, striving and choosing), vocation, personal choice, and spiritual definition. The next set of pages attempts to identify common myths that distract would-be adults as they contemplate the movement to maturity. The final section of this book explores the pastoral care of persons in this transition as they experience the challenges of confusing options, unclear identity, late adolescence, commitment deferment, dysfunctional family messages, vocational choices, and "spiritual winters" on their way to adulthood. An addendum to the study will suggest ways in which institutions of learning, including the church, may empower, enrich, and bless the journey of young adults.

Section 1

All Dressed Up and No Place to Go?

Today's new adult has grown up in a culture that has been steadily redefining personal identity. Gone are the days of assumed gender stereotypes and clear delineations by task or role. Today men cook, and women run corporations; males are perceived as nurturers, and women are known as task-oriented managers. The days when "men were men and boys were boys," as Archie Bunker used to sing on the popular television program *All in the Family*, are no longer around.

A major challenge of adolescence is that of developing a sense of self while still living with one's family of origin. Teenagers inherit a set of genes and a ritual of behaviors from the families in which they grow up. They must next begin a gradual (or abrupt)

movement away from their families in order to define and identify
their own personhood. The biblical description of Jacob leaving
his parents and brother and heading toward an uncertain adventure is a model of today's young adult seekers—all dressed up and
knowing little about where they're going.

The biblical sketch of this young adult leaving home (Gen 28)
to start an independent life contains several issues familiar to
today's late adolescent. Jacob is on a journey *toward* a new place to
live—but also *away* from the way he has lived. He is a young man
leaving his family of beginnings and searching for a new set of
people with whom he can belong. He is a man with a fuzzy dream
about the future, and a man who has no clear picture of what the
future will look like. Jacob is a "vision hunter," pausing along the
journey to spend the night—trying to gain a clearer sight of what
he's looking for. His overnight stop at Beth-El is not accidental.
Nothing he does at that religious sanctuary is without purpose: an
ancient belief held that a person seeking a vision from the God of
the place could go to one of the sacred spots where God had
appeared to others (and therefore designated a "holy place"), take
a stone from the altar of sacrifice, and place it under their head
while they rested or slept—so that the god of that region might
come to them in a dream or vision and reveal some mystery or
purpose in their life.

So Jacob in Genesis follows the behaviors of the ancient
believers, seeking out a sanctuary, using a stone from the altar as a
pillow, and inviting the god of the sacred place to reveal himself to
the sleeper. The young pilgrim, incidentally, expected to hear from
a new god, since the understanding of his day was that each god
had control over only a certain limited territory. Jacob, having
crossed the border beyond the boundaries of his father's God,

anticipated a vision from another god who had made no covenants with his father. Jacob's surprise, captured in his comment, "surely Yahweh was in this place, and I knew it not," (Gen 28:18, KJV), is not a statement about being surprised that a god was present in that place, but surprised that *the same God of his father* (Yahweh) was present and starting a conversation in that sacred space!

Jacob was both excited and afraid. The adventure of a new beginning, on his own, was certainly attractive. The loneliness of being on his own must also have been partly terrifying. The reality of *being unknown* was, however, probably his greatest fear. Lurking in the deeper layers of what the psalmist calls his "secret heart" (Ps 51:6), Jacob knew that he was an unknown quantity to himself. He did not know himself. Like many older teenagers and adults in their early twenties, Jacob had spent most of his life doing what someone else told him to do and believing what someone else had said about him. He only knew what others knew about him. He had not heard his own voice; he had not found a voice inside he could clearly call his own.

Jacob, like other tentative adults, suspected the promptings and voices inside of him as possibly messages others had made *for* him. He had not yet identified what he was after, or who he was, or who he was choosing to become. He had grown up accepting what children naturally do first in families: they follow their parents' directions, actions, and choices. Eventually, however, children wean themselves from this dependence and begin to assert their own thoughts, choices, and behaviors.

Quite naturally, the first self-assertions and personal choices of adolescents are often made in *reaction* to parental choices or values, not as original responses initiated in the absence of outside intimations. Jacob's behaviors prior to his exit from home suggest

a series of reactions to members of his family rather than a
sequence of choices prompted by a free mind: Out of response to
a long-felt sense of competition with Esau, Jacob chooses to entice
his brother to surrender his own birthright. He deceives his father
Isaac over an inheritance out of jealousy over Isaac's favoritism
toward Esau. He conspires with his mother to leave home out of
fear for his safety—not out of a desire to follow a dream. His
overnight stay at Beth-El is clear evidence that he *had* no dream
and was seeking one. He is a young man who does not know himself. Like the seeking young adult of today, his first conversation is
with himself. He will soon begin to give birth to his own sense of
identity.

Identity: Getting to Know Oneself for the First Time

Jacob's restless venture mirrors the discomfort of young adults
today wanting to affirm a personal identity—and not knowing
what they can affirm. Elizabeth O'Connor, describing the dual
dimension of a personal journey every individual must make, several years ago identified two paths she called the *Journey Inward,
Journey Outward* (New York: Harper & Row, 1975). In a book
designed to assist members of the Church of the Savior in
Washington D.C., she advocated the discipline of self-reflection
and self-understanding as prerequisites to any vocation or service.
In order to give ourselves to any task or purpose, we must first, she
declared, come to know ourselves.

Young people in the twenty-first century have grown up in a
society that encourages them to do the opposite. If author Neil

Postman is correct, the immediate past two generations have been reared in an environment that fosters distraction from self-investigation (*Amusing Ourselves to Death* [New York: Penguin Books, 2005]). Postman suggests that our American subculture has worked overtime to produce gadgets, games, and exercises designed to remove us from the experience of self-discovery. He argues that we live in a society that spends a lot of energy trying to entertain itself and that we devote time and effort (even on vacation!) to ensure that we avoid reflection and self-awareness.

The subculture of late adolescence plays directly into this avoidance. Young people are inclined to dress alike, sound alike, and act enough alike so that they will not "stand out" as different. The outward appearance camouflages a need for individuality. Even everyday communication is essentially superficial, so that the young person rarely takes a "journey inward." Such behaviors are not peculiar to teenagers, but add to the individual's lack of awareness of his or her unique identity, since self-distinction is blurred in favor of "being like" everyone else the same age. How does a young person discover selfhood when so regularly encouraged toward uniformity and "group think"?

Mood swings add to the bewilderment of self-discovery, for hormones, physical changes, emotional surges, and self-doubt alter personal perceptions. What a young person might sense at one moment gives way to the unpredictable preference of another mood. Choices and affirmations can change dramatically during late adolescence, making any stable sense of who we are and what we like very tentative. By the time young adults reach their early twenties, they have experienced enough mood changes to question the validity of any self-perceptions, or the reliability of any personal impressions.

Self-image at this time is a crucial variable that plays havoc with personal identity. Most young adults carry enough low self-esteem from adolescence to last them a lifetime. Brief but lasting painful moments experienced as children or as teenagers have a profound effect on self-image. Many young adults not only don't know themselves well, but, in addition, don't like what they *do* know about themselves—inaccurate as it may be.

Much of young people's self-image is based on an inaccurate collection of myths that begins to define them in their own minds. The quest for a healthy personal identity too often dissolves in a conflicting array of contradictory and confusing messages about the self. Nurtured by family members and other significant persons, the young adult has gathered a sizable portion of what Gordon Allport called "secondhand fittings," or borrowed beliefs and notions about oneself (see his *The Individual & His Religion* [New York: MacMillan Co., 1950).

This haphazard assembly of amassed perceptions of oneself by others needs sorting out and evaluating, since it is secondhand material. At some point in life, every human being needs to begin the task of defining himself or herself apart from the "hand-me-down" images and definitions of others. Beyond the inherited characteristics over which no one has control (up to now), each person must come to terms with what he chooses to affirm and embrace as his own definition of self. We must intentionally decide what and who we shall become—or we will float aimlessly from novelty to novelty.

Such important choices and definitions need time and energy to develop, and late adolescence and early adulthood are the designated seasons when such investigation and discovery take place. It is an investigation, first of all, because each person must take initiative to explore the intricate and hidden dimension of the personal self. It is a discovery, on the other hand, because the seeker is also exploring an unknown personal territory that is waiting to be found. The challenge for the young adult, for the family, and for the church is to acknowledge and to bless this self-discovery with enthusiasm and patience. The family and the church have often shown the enthusiasm but faltered in providing patience in this crucial sacred task.

How can family and institutions of learning help young people in this fragile personal quest? These two human families can offer safety and support for youth as they pursue personal identity by providing a fallow atmosphere in which four avenues of development may take place in each person's journey toward identity. These highways on which they create self-definition all contribute to the discovery of the image of God in each individual and are an essential part of the human journey. They include spaces for imagining (dreaming), exploring (seeking), striving (wrestling), and choosing (selecting).

Imagining and Dreaming a Self

Imagining

Young people need time to do what we call "daydreaming," an important mental exercise in which we try on ideas, perceptions, and dreams "for fit." According to one therapist (and father of two late adolescents at the time), three of the central exercises that develop a sense of self in youth are the capacity to imagine, to dream, and to seek (Wayne E. Oates, *On Becoming Children of God* [The Westminster Press, 1966]).

Unfortunately, much of the content of this internal conversation often turns negatively upon the self, because older adolescents put themselves down in the process of reviewing collected messages and memories. They thus develop a reality all their own—even though their impressions are rarely based on accurate perceptions. These regular "internal" conversations (called "scripts" by communication experts) exert a formative effect on negative adolescent self-identity. An important exercise for individual, family, and church is to regularly monitor these internal messages so that the emerging adult may arrive into young adulthood with a more realistic—and positive—sense of self.

Being made in the image of God involves several inherent capacities, not the least of which is "imagining." The young adult working on identity can begin to develop a sense of being a "separate self" in the same way that children gradually develop a sense of themselves as separate beings from their primary caregivers. Psychologist Erik Erikson (in *Childhood and Society* [New York: W.W. Norton, 1963]), among others, helped us understand that an infant eventually experiences herself as a person *apart from* other persons. This self-awareness is gradual but significant, and a child's first negative declarations ("No!") are actually positive affirmations of "seeing" (imaging themselves as a separate entity from other entities).

Imagining requires time and energy. The growth stage that requires high levels of "imaging work" begins during the teenage years. The daydreaming that adolescents generate is an exercise in such purposive reflections. Like the apparent "at random" movements of an infant in the crib (which we now know are the child's response to the rhythm in the mother's voice), the reflective exercises teenagers usually undertake are unrehearsed attempts to reach within themselves and touch chords of personal definition. Teenagers go to their rooms (their private spaces), listen to music by themselves, and create moments in which they can "just veg," i.e., spend time doing unrecorded thinking.

Our society regularly discourages such activity, preferring to label reflection as "idle" or useless behavior. Adolescents use such private emotional spaces to practice the art of self-imagination. Adults often misunderstand the hard work in which small children engage when they "play" and fail to register the amount of learning (about four times as much as an average adult) taking place during early playtime. Late adolescent daydreaming is also regularly misunderstood. When a young person uses time to imagine and reflect, she is expending significant amounts of energy "learning" about herself. Difficult as it is to measure, the work and insight that occurs in those private moments is central to the business of shaping a personal identity.

The young person who spends time looking at himself in the mirror is pursuing the art of "imagining himself." Anyone who has lived with a teenager knows how important "looks" are to these emerging adults. Time spent in front of the mirror is easily matched by the struggle either to "look" like other teenagers or to react by looking unlike anything parents or peers expect. The inner drive to disguise themselves to join the "mass" of what their peers look like is accentuated by the anxiety that someone may place them in a role before they themselves have found their own script.

Imagining also takes the form of "image worship." New heroes are selected during these years, models who evoke the fantasy of what young people might become or think they would like to be. Such fantasies are regulated by the reassurance that we are not, in fact, who our heroes are, for these heroes might change—or any of us ourselves might feel trapped into a script we fear we may not permanently wish.

Imagination is both an exercise and an art. We are born with the capacity to imagine, which involves creativity and vision. As children we were often encouraged to use our creative capacities and other times discouraged from doing so. School activities and disciplines both allow and squelch the use of imagination. Adults often ask children what they want to be "when they grow up." Children are encouraged to imagine, to "try things on for size," and usually are given no restrictions or boundaries to their visions. As emerging adults, however, new limitations are placed on our imagining. Test results in school give us a measure of our capabilities for certain enterprises and vocations. Family and friends offer suggestions that relate to our aptitudes (and *their* preferences). The difficulty of seeing ourselves for the first time as an adult adds to the self-imposed restrictions we place on our imagination.

One of the main challenges to employing our imagination resides in our capacity to "image" aspects of ourselves. By the time an adolescent begins to tap into the accumulated, internalized images he has of himself, he also has stored away a variety of messages that restrict self-definition. In place already are messages about self-worth, perceptions from the family of origin, and "scripts" or roles both family and community have ascribed to them. Many of these borrowed messages (myths) are inaccurate and misleading. The capacity to imagine ourselves in particular futures is highly dependent on our ability to "inhabit" those scenarios or roles. Self-esteem plays a major function in our capacity to visualize ourselves doing certain things and following specific identities.

Parents, in their eagerness to convey a proper sense of self-worth to their children, have sometimes added to the problem by communicating that the youth "can do anything she wants to." Such general messages regarding multiple abilities are inoffensive exaggerations during childhood but oppressive and inaccurate representations in late adolescence and early adulthood.

How can we tap into the wonderfully under-explored exercise of imagination? We can begin by giving young adults *permission* to spend time doing just that. We need time and energy to imagine the world within us, just as children need opportunities to explore the world around them. Several actions foster such investigation. The activity of reading books, seeing plays, and watching movies is one such exercise in imagining. We read and see ourselves into the pages and actions of someone else's life, all the time "trying on" certain characteristics and aspects of others—to see if they "fit" us.

Spending intentional time alone also feeds the engine of imagination. We choose to be alone during various times of the day or week, but rarely interpret such moments as active ingredients in the recipe of self-discovery. Time alone is essential for self-understanding. We need to acknowledge the value and importance of personal reflection by ourselves. We need to give ourselves time away from others as a personal dialogue with ourselves. Folks who develop the capacity to schedule time by themselves discover thoughts and perceptions within themselves that are worthy of attention. Rather than consider such private moments as wasted time or "selfish" withdrawals, we can celebrate what students of the human soul call some of the sacred conversations with ourselves.

We need not analyze or record such conversations—nor take them literally. The freedom to imagine, by definition, requires neither boundaries nor controlling "rules of engagement." As such, imagining or daydreaming may occur with silence, with music, and with conversations with oneself. The inner dialogue of wondering what we shall become, and dreaming the possibilities, is a valuable ritual for adolescents and young adults.

Some people take the time to journal their thoughts and dreams regularly. Some young people find time alone in order to collect their thoughts. The emerging adult sometimes fills life with so much activity that private, solitary time is hard to find. Adolescents often carve out such private moments by placing a set of earphones on their heads and drowning out the noises around them. Some people like to run or jog regularly by themselves, an exercise that gives them space and privacy for a few moments each day. For others, even the pursuit of a hobby may provide some quiet, personal "downtime." The method chosen is less important than saving time each day for personal reflection, daydreaming, and imagining.

Imagining also engages our unique capacity to think and create on our own. The gift of imagination equips us to construct our own thoughts. Our sense of being a true self emerges in our awareness that we have the power—and the capacity—to have a thought no one else has and to own that thought as uniquely ours. To form an identity is to begin the process of acknowledging our power to function as a person with thoughts that belong to us alone.

Having an identity also means creating our own thoughts, images, and pictures of self. The capacity to think is the power to create—and in creating our own world of ideas, notions, and perceptions, we create a self that is all ours. In order to begin accepting this gift of uniqueness, each of us must at some point "separate" from the other identities around us. That is why adolescents must create some emotional—and often physical—distance, from their parents and/or family of origin. Such distancing often generates anxiety and concern in the family from whom they are "separating," who misread such actions as rejection.

A mature community of faith can offer specific help in the ongoing dialogue of imagination. A youth group that takes its members seriously can spend time with a late adolescent answering the questions, "Who do you think I am?" or "What do you see me doing?" Without condemning a member of the group to a certain stereotype, young people who experience an emerging adult in various settings can contribute to the pool of "imagined" perceptions and the possibilities lying ahead.

Dreaming

Imagining a self also requires dreaming. Most adults think of dreaming as serendipitous night fantasies that invade our sleep at unexpected times. Although dreams belong to the sleeping hours, they also belong to the waking hours. Imagining as a mental exercise engages the human capacity to fantasize. Late adolescents and young adults must conjecture and imagine possible futures in their lives created during the fully conscious hours of the day—in their mind's eye. As the prophet Joel said, "afterward I will pour out my spirit on all flesh, your sons and your daughters shall prophesy, your old men shall dream dreams, and your young men shall see visions" (Joel 2:28).

For the young adult, the need to apprehend a dream, or vision, of what they may become, is an essential task in personal development. Every person needs to dream a future—in fact, several futures. The God of many talents, whose Spirit is at work in each emerging adult, creates more dreams and options than anyone need employ. This God of a free mind and free imagination, in addition, is a God of many choices. Young people will dream many dreams and only choose a few. The capacity to dream and to envision oneself in several possible scenarios is a rich and challenging invitation.

The richness for personal development during this season resides in the many possible dreams of young adults. The challenge resides in the selection of which dreams to follow. A central function of late adolescence and young adulthood is to take the time *to dream several possible selves and several possible futures.* Confusing though such multiple visions may be, they are in number characteristic of the God who created every creature as God is—multitalented. These "multiple fantasies of the future" are the dream of a God who wished all creatures abundant freedom and choice.

Dreaming is another arena in which adolescents imagine. Daydreaming and night dreaming are both intentional and accidental. Like Jacob, people can "plan" to dream by setting aside time for reflection, choosing spaces where dreaming can best occur, and finding opportunities for entertaining thoughts about themselves and the future. Dreaming is "accidental" in that it may also occur in unplanned moments, as when a thought develops that invites further reflection, or an event captures our imagination, as we say. Unscheduled dreaming is serendipitous, an unrehearsed discovery of an idea or insight that takes us by surprise and provides an insight.

Dreaming and imagining require time and opportunity. If imagining and daydreaming are, in fact, useful exercises, they deserve intentional moments and opportunities to develop. The

Western culture has, unfortunately, only lately valued this art of meditation and reflection so common in other cultures. Eastern mysticism and several "Old World" religions have long championed the importance of mental review and have set aside time and energy for the development of nurtured thought and focused reverie.

In the absence of such "mental spaces," our society has devised other rituals to assist adolescents in finding their own space. Some of these "private moments" appear in our daily and weekly schedules, and some of them lie hidden in the assignments of first employments. The mindless jobs some young people take allow them the luxury of spacing out at work. The unusual late hours some young adults keep provide them with personal time for free association and boundless mental explorations. Time spent listening to music or watching television employs many leisure moments for daydreaming. Even the car trip over the weekend or the outdoor jaunt with a friend offer potential journeys into the inner world of fantasies about the future and who we are becoming.

Work assignments also buy us time for self-discovery. Some young people join the military for the structured schedule it provides, leaving them room to fallow or dream their personal identity without any pressure to make important choices about the future quickly. Popular forms of higher education (college, tech school, apprenticeships) also provide a moratorium that postpones the necessity of defining personal identity. More than 50 percent of college graduates in this country pursue goals totally unrelated to their declared "major" in college, confirming the practical reality that higher education stretches and matures the individual but does not necessarily prepare them for a specific vocation.

These "filler" jobs equip us with several valuable advantages. Looking busy appears responsible and removes significant pressure society places on us to look productive. Jobs and educational activities also give us an explanation for what we are currently doing with our lives and even provide distracting clues about our emerging identities. Anyone who has had to explain their major to an inquisitive friend or tell someone what they are doing now knows the value of a filler activity. Such jobs and study projects provide us activities during the time we need to "tread water" as we work on the recipe of self-definition.

Mental health professionals have for years identified a season in personal development in which young adults take a quiet "time-out" to catch up personally with themselves. Called a "moratorium" (from the Latin word *moratorium*, a delay), this personal space when time is suspended gives young people an opportunity to catch up emotionally and spiritually with their physical progress. Years ago a friend who grew up in Nigeria told me of taking a long journey on foot with a childhood Nigerian friend. As they crossed over a mountainous area, the native companion suddenly stopped and came to his knees as if catching his breath. My friend turned around to ask him why he had stopped, since the Nigerian was in good physical condition and showed no signs of fatigue. The kneeling companion replied, "I'm waiting for my soul to catch up with my body!"

A psychological (or personal) moratorium is youth's way of slowing down so that their "soul" (self) may catch up with an emerging adult body. There are many different ways in which we take a moratorium in order to buy time in the journey of personal development. In our North American society, institutions of learning and congregations provide the individual with an environment and an opportunity to take time out emotionally and spiritually.

Exploring: Seeking a Self

Young people not only need the freedom to dream a self unhindered, they also need the opportunity to explore a self. The young adult of today needs methods and means of seeking clues to his identity. The exploration of his inner world requires markers and signposts. Mapping out the content of our identity takes time and work. Such exploration needs initiative and guidance.

A useful place for young adults to begin such personal investigation is by examining the history of their own families. None of us are creatures "invented on the spot." We are the products (and the dreams) of several generations, and we contain the genes (the DNA) that identify us as members of families with their own identities and characteristics. We have a rich assortment of sources in our family histories, and there are several ways to learn something about ourselves by studying the families from which we came.

One favorite way of studying such personal histories is called a "genogram," an exercise in which we "map out" in a diagram the different members of our families for three or more generations. This exercise is accomplished by interviewing family members as a means of identifying the various branches of our family trees. Such investigation involves a set of conversations with as many members of the family as we can reach. The exploration identifies the ages and order of birth for each family member on both sides of the family and establishes how they were related to the family and what their vocation was. Thus persons deceased and living, married, divorced, or single, in whatever birth order they appeared, engage the seeking young adult in a dialogue that begins to tell the seeker something about who he or she is.

Jewish families have practiced such "identifications" through the art of storytelling, as they use specific religious celebrations to narrate the story of the origin of their family. Such traditions employ rich recounting of the family history, back several generations, and often provide the children and youth in the family with a sense of their own identities through connecting with the story of their family. Other families share special occasions in which they "retell" some of the family experiences that give definition and identity to the assembled listeners. Family stories help define the individuals who belong in each family.

Young adults can also reach into the "reservoir" of family stories they have collected over the years. The favorite events and stories of the family in which we grew up are of value in the formation and understanding of a personal sense of self. Family gatherings often become the occasion for such storytelling. The informal assembly of family members over a holiday inspires the retelling of the "family myths," the larger-than-life restating of personal experiences in the lives of family members.

Special occasions create an atmosphere for such "retelling." In many American families, the death of a loved one prompts an interchange of memories and comments during the ritual of a funeral. Family members who have not seen each other for years come together to share in the loss and review their own past and present in conversations inspired by the conclusion of one person's "story"—the death of a particular loved one.

Seeking: The World Within

If dreaming and imagining are "inside" journeys, seeking is both internal and external. We begin the "search for a self" by listening to the voices inside of us. Seeking means an active investigation of what we have discovered within us and the voices and options outside us that give "feet" to our journey of discovery. Seeking means trying out some of the abilities and promptings inside of us by looking for ways in which they can be expressed. Seeking means turning over stones in our personal collection of skills and predilections to see what our discoveries mean. Seeking involves initiative and engagement. Seeking means the active pursuit of hints and possibilities that attract us. Seeking is "digging" to explore what certain preferences mean.

Seeking, no doubt, means exploring the world inside of us we've discovered so far. The unknown preferences and predilections each individual possesses become clearer as adolescence blooms. We begin to note certain repetitive patterns in choices we make. We notice that we prefer some activities over others. We choose to spend time in certain ways. Family and friends tend to use particular adjectives to describe us. A pattern emerges that begins to define us apart from others.

Nowadays we have several practical tests that help us identify some of these preferences we display. School counselors and vocational engineers provide clues into the "inner nature" of each adolescent and young adult. One of the most popular ways to describe personal characteristics is that of psychologist Carl Jung and his followers. Jung identified a set of eight "preferences" that guide the understanding of personality: He noted that people tend either to be energized and stimulated more by the presence of people (extraversion) or by things (introversion). Some prefer to follow facts and concrete reality (sensing), as opposed to the abstract and the theoretical (intuition). Some tend toward the logical and skeptic inquiry (thinking) in preference to the emotional and the accepting (feeling). Finally, we choose between methodical, routine, and closure (judging), and the spontaneous and open-ended (perceiving). Jung and followers were later assisted in this personality identification quest by a twosome called Myers and Briggs, who elicited from the above preferences a set of letters to identify sixteen major "personality type" clusters (ENFJ, ISTP, etc.).

When such written exercises have been used to give some clarity to individual taste and behavior preferences, they have been useful to the seeker. Other questionnaires also aid in the identification of personal predilections and traits. Specialists are trained to interpret such practical written evaluations as the Johnson Temperament Scale, the Kuder Personal Preference Inventory, and the Strong Vocational Interest Test. Many vocational schools and other institutions offer interpretation of such tests and can often assist the seeker in identifying a cluster of skills, personal preferences, and recurring themes in an individual profile.

Seeking: The World Without

Employed adults are another important resource for the seeking youth. A circle of family friends, the family itself, and communities of faith all provide a rich source of valuable and available vocational models "at work." People at their jobs offer insight on work choice, personality preferences, and identity development. The now well-known "take your child to work day" that many businesses and places of employment support is a stimulating on-site opportunity for a young person to experience a work setting, observe a vocation, and ask questions about particular choices individuals have made that helped them understand their identities and find their jobs.

Congregations can assist such investigations by providing regular "workshops" in which young people can visit adults in "job fairs" and learn something from these living sources who have had earlier personal journeys and vocational choices. Institutions of learning and communities of faith have an available platform where members of the institution may regularly be invited to share their vocational journeys. Universities and seminaries would do well to provide opportunities for healthy adult vocational models to sketch their own stories for the benefit of emerging adults. The local church is an ideal setting in which the rich resource of seasoned adults may offer an ongoing dialogue with young people on such matters of identity, choice, vocation, and work exploration.

Another contribution in "shadowing" people we admire is that in doing so, young people learn what their heroes actually do. By observing certain persons in their daily routine, youth can visualize what it might be like to be in their shoes. "Studying" other people gives us a concrete means of imagining what it would be like to live and work as they do. A careful look at the daily experiences of others gives the emerging adult a chance to shed any romanticized notions about what being an adult is like, what a particular occupation is like, or how a certain kind of person lives.

One additional dimension of the adult vocational model deserves attention. Institutions and congregations contain a wealth of mentors who could be assigned to youth periodically for a "covenant of personal formation." Such a mentoring relationship involves a tangible commitment by an adult to spend time with a young person—for a specific amount of time—in order to provide a concrete model of adult identity and vocation. Young people in late adolescence need adults other than their parents to whom they can look as healthy examples of adult development.

How else may young people seek? Seeking obviously involves taking initiative, and such a journey requires effort and action. Christ's comment in the seventh chapter of Matthew (7:7-11) describes the nature of such continuous activity by carefully employing three different verbs in a particular way. The Greek tense (the imperative) in each case should translate the following way: "Keep on asking, and you will receive; keep on seeking, and you will find; keep on knocking, and it shall be opened. . . ." The young adult has an active role to play in his quest for identity and focus. He or she participates in the exploration of life and the future by continuously asking questions, seeking options, and knocking on each door that appears along the way.

Such engaged pursuit can be tiring, and a failure to come up with quick answers or results can be discouraging—particularly for a young person. If Gore Vidal, an American writer and critic, is correct about the culture in which we live, the average young adult has been immersed in "the idolatry of the immediate and the superficial." If she has learned to believe only in quick results, or has learned little of postponed gratification, our seeker may soon despair. There are even persons in an individual's local congregation who will imply that immediate answers always come to people of faith, leaving the bewildered seeker with the impression that if he finds or receives little at first, he is not only confused or lost but also a person of minimal faith. Little wonder that some late adolescents wind up leaving their local churches, convinced that the God they knew has either abandoned them or is punishing them with silence.

Seeking takes patience. Like my brother and I trying to turn up the heat on a cake recipe to make the cake ready faster, young people become anxious and want to rush the answer when they feel off-balanced or unfocused. Sometimes we need to remind them that Jesus Christ was thirty years old before he began a "serious" vocation. Anxiety can often lead the clueless young adult to make unwise or ill-advised decisions, one of which is to conclude that faith is of little use in this uncharted journey. This is a time when developing an understanding of *mystery* and *waiting* as important ingredients to faith can be of significant value. The church and the pastor who helps youth understand the role of mystery in life will provide young people much hope and a deeper understanding of faith. Likewise, the community of faith that can assist late adolescents or young adults in discovering the importance of waiting as a valuable experience in life will have contributed richly both to their faith and to their understanding of life, reality, and purpose.

Seeking is a continuous search for helpful clues and useful directions in the journey of identity and vocation. Pursuing and gathering those pieces in the "puzzle of life" is essential—and often hard work. Little is worthwhile without the effort to get it, and every discovered ingredient in the recipe for personal understanding and life purpose is valuable material.

Wrestling: Striving

Exploring and discovering one's life purpose involves dreaming, imagining, seeking, and searching, but it also requires striving. Effort and search assume some active struggle with reality. Like

Jacob wrestling with his angel, each pilgrim on the road to adulthood must face obstacles and challenges. Examination and pursuit
not only require effort, but the struggle of facing challenges in life.
The journey toward maturity is sometimes an uphill climb, and
more effort is required. Some choices we make will be temporary;
some pursuits will prove unfruitful; some experiments will result
in elimination.

With few exceptions, young adults assume school and work
assignments with little sense that they are making long-term commitments. They hope, in fact, that they will not be held to their
momentary choices for long. Responding to the tentative nature
of their vocational signals, they continue to seek jobs that will provide them some temporary security and freedom while allowing
them to pursue the undefined promptings that continue to stir
within them.

That is why a primary posture of late adolescence is that of
striving. Aware that something important about themselves has
not yet been found, young adults of today are most often on an
uneasy quest. The mystery that lures them on is the attraction of
self-discovery. The search is constant, if irregular. The fuzzy nature
of their goals makes any discovery a challenge. The anxiety that
persists is in *not* finding what is being sought, in missing what is
desired, and in waiting for what has not appeared—and wondering if it will.

The importance of the find, however, makes *seeking* an important exercise, even if its momentary result is repetitiously
disappointing. "Striving" is the word we use to describe the nervous energy and restlessness that accompany the pursuit of
self-definition and vocational discovery at this age. There is no
timetable or schedule that can guarantee success or discovery by a

certain date. There are no predictable behaviors or motions that can promise results. The journey and the disappointments go hand in hand.

This undefined struggle creates its own discouragement. As unclear and vague as it suggests, this active pursuit is both to define a self and to choose one's life work. Such exertion in young adulthood is a "hit and miss" adventure. The seeking has an objective, but the road to its discovery is quite nebulous. In a society and work environment that measure results concretely, such generalized pursuit eludes definition and creates unsteady moments and uneasy questions: Is the quest realistic? Can such unclear goals be recognized? Is the pursuit a waste of time? How does one go about making progress in this exploration? What are the signs to look for? How long will the journey take? These and other questions challenge the searching pilgrim. The search is often a struggle.

For this reason, the nature of young adulthood assumes a certain restlessness that is never completely quieted. There is at the heart of any personal quest a constant tension, a struggle with things as they are, and a yearning for the undiscovered and the as yet not revealed. Such a station in life requires constant management of unfocused anxiety, for a nervous tension stirs just beneath the surface. Hence the sense that young people have of wrestling with life itself, of struggling with every decision that defines or delineates any boundaries for the self.

This strenuous activity of struggling with choices, events, opportunities, and ideas requires a lot of energy. Young adults expend significant amounts of energy wrestling with a dream, an identity, and a vocation. The struggle to give definition to ourselves is a labor-intensive process. Sometimes the struggle is positive and exhilarating; on other occasions the struggle and the pursuit are difficult and exhausting.

Striving, realistically, must acknowledge the strain and toil required in "wrestling." Some of the struggle is inevitable and necessary. Like the strain required of the body in trying to run a race, the energy and stress involved in the active pursuit of personal development, identity, and vocational focus is vital. Striving is a positive investment of the self in the pursuit of purpose. Some of the strife and struggle has benefits. Some of the wrestling is negative. None of the effort is without some pain.

What aspects of the struggle are positive, and which are negative? Straining to reflect on the many different options and dimensions of the self contributes to the process of examining and affirming a self. Like heat to a motor, such reflective straining is useful up to a point. If the reflection and thoughtful evaluation become too intense, preoccupation and worry take the place of concern and constructive inquiry. Ruminating over events or issues can consume so much energy and attention that the exercise can become destructive. Repetitive reflection without boundaries results in a paralyzing preoccupation or an obsessive thought pattern that offers no help and creates frustration and defeat. Worry is a circular thought process that has no benefit, for it works on the assumption that the constant review of an issue from the same point of view will lead to its quick resolution. In the chapters ahead, we shall discuss how worry is fueled by a heightened anxiety that seeks immediate relief. Heightened anxiety is the same as excessive heat to an engine: rather than add to its performance, excessive heat (anxiety) leads to a diminished operating capacity (meltdown!) and, consequently, to the opposite of resolution.

Such anxiety also fuels premature decisions and ill-advised choices, made hastily in an attempt to reduce the discomfort of stress.

Reflection, therefore, must employ some useful boundaries. By setting a limit to the amount of time we use for "thinking" about an issue, we can engage the positive side of striving without allowing it to control us. When reflection becomes worry, it controls our energy, affects our perspective, and contributes mainly to a sense of defeat and discomfort.

Striving also mobilizes energy and motivation for the engagement of a task. When trying on a job or an idea, taking a self-preference test, or working a dream, the energy expended adds to the process of discovery. "Strivers" are active seekers who employ their resources and capacities in the pursuit of their goals. The act of striving is, in fact, the experience of action as opposed to inaction. The seeking young person who is "stirring" and striving after something experiences the sensation of participating in the resolution of his need. Unlike the passive individual who sees herself as waiting and uninvolved in "doing something," the striving young person savors the investment of "working" on the discovery she wishes to make—in a tangible way.

Lewis Sherrill, describing the human exercise of engaging life as a challenge, called such striving a "saga"(see his *The Struggle of the Soul* [New York: MacMillan Co., 1951]). Explaining that human beings tend to adopt one of three postures in the pursuit of life's meaning, he identified those approaches as "treadmill," "saga," and "pilgrimage." According to Lewis, people in the first posture tend to experience life primarily as a circular event that repeats itself with little sense of progress. Much like the Greeks described history as repeating itself over and over, "treadmill" persons tend to think of their human journey largely in terms of repetitive events. "Saga" persons, on the other hand, tend to respond to life discoveries primarily as an uphill battle to be won. For such people, life is a constant challenge and conquest, ever moving forward, always pressing the discoverer to fight for gained territory—always pushing the seeker back. The journey of "pilgrimage," again by contrast, is that of life as a movement forward, making progress, and gaining ground through growth and discovery—neither in a circular nor a combative way.

Life for young people at times will seem circular, like a treadmill. Every inquiry and unclear conclusion will appear at first as a repetitive encounter, with no progress. Youth will also experience life as an upward battle, a never-ending challenge, a struggle to conquer, and a striving to reach more. Action and reaction describe the nature of discovery—for a while. Straining to gain ground may seem like an endless battle. Some of the journey involves struggle, fight, and conquest. And, properly lived, the struggles and the fight can give birth to strength and conviction. Like the butterfly that must strain and stretch to free itself from its cocoon, youth who struggle and strain with dreams, identity, and vocation are also gaining strength in their wings when they do so. Soon they will fly.

Striving offers two additional contributions to the journey of a young person: The first one is the "action" effect striving produces in the individual. Like exercise improving the work and growth of muscles, striving is a physical, emotional, and spiritual activity that stretches and tones the young person. Engaged and striving young people are busy people, pursuing their hopes and dreams in a manner that connects them with life. As opposed to being idle, the young adult who is stirring and wrestling is developing strength for life's journey, pushing herself and stimulating her selfhood to exceed her former boundaries. The striving young adult is a growing young adult.

Secondly, such struggle also contributes a steady dose of confidence to the young and fragile emerging identity of a person. With each experiment and struggle, the young person gains confidence in himself and in his future. Experience and effort contribute to a growing sense of assurance within the person that he is *capable*. On the negative side, a regular dose of defeats and bad experiences can undermine a youth's sense of confidence. Families and faith groups should watch for the irregular string of poor experiences that disillusion and discourage young seekers.

Choosing: Selecting

The young must dream and imagine; they must seek and strive; and they must eventually also choose and decide. The journey of self-definition has a place for imagining without being confined to first imaginings. The road also provides for searching that is for a while unclear and undefined. The movement to adulthood has its moments of struggle and striving, even waiting, when the road and way are unclear. But each of these steps must someday give way to choice and selection in order for a young person to affirm self-definition and focus.

Choice and freedom themselves breed confusion and anxiety. Choice requires selection and the possible elimination of options. Freedom with purpose requires responsibility and accountability, and such options usually include some degree of confidence and risk. Along the journey to adulthood, some dreams must be laid aside. Some of the searching will lead to dead ends. Even the striving and struggling will eliminate some of the options. Some of the choices we make may be only for a season. Eventually, some choices become more permanent.

One sign of maturity is the capacity to choose, to will one thing or two over many, to select one path over several paths. An additional challenge on the road to adulthood, then, is the place or moment when we declare certain choices. At some point, some dreams are chosen as ours—for a longer journey. Some of the seeking will affirm certain "finds" as central to our identities. A few of the struggles will produce specific affirmations. The individual's identity and vocation will then begin to emerge.

Such choices do not always come easy, but they are necessary. Dreaming and seeking are valuable intermediate exercises to the acquisition of a particular sense of identity. They contribute to the self-discovery that every human being must undertake. Like "warm-up" activities in preparation for a race, each of the experiences identified earlier in these pages (dreaming and imagining, seeking, striving and wrestling) are preparation for the "main event": the time when a person assumes certain principles as her own and claims a specific definition as her identity. Such declarations come only after much inquiry and investigation; but they must eventually replace the tentative format each of us has constructed as a "proposed identity." Otherwise, all of us would drift from dream to dream, never defining ourselves. The dreaming, the searching, and the struggling all belong in the vocational closet of garments "tried on for size," but not necessarily bought. Eventually, some defining "garments" must be owned as ours.

Late adolescence was designed precisely for such initial investigation and inquiry. Adulthood, on the other hand, requires definition—buying the garments and beginning to wear them as ours. Even if the choices made are beginning affirmations, choosing must eventually take place. Adults may still choose again. Adulthood offers recurring opportunities for self-definition. But the movement from late adolescence to adulthood is punctuated by the invitations—and someday the capacity—to affirm a particular self after a journey of investigation. At some point, then, after imagining a self, dreaming a future or two, and searching and struggling with several options, the individual on a journey to adulthood makes some decisions. He decides what's most important to him; he decides who he wants to be; and he decides what he wants to do.

Wayne E. Oates once called this step "taming your dreams." He explained that all of us collect a variety of dreams in childhood and adolescence and that part of growing up is discarding and setting aside the dreams that don't fit. "Taming," to him, was the exercise of whittling our fantasies to the size of "doable" dreams (see his *On Becoming Children of God* [Philadelphia: The Westminster Press, 1966]). Children and young people have the luxury of imagining themselves in "larger-than-life" scenarios. Adulthood involves the wisdom of "taming" unrealistic expectations to their proper sizes. The difference between a fantasy and a dream is that the first has to do with "unreal" possibilities, while the second is a vision of a realistic probability. Some childhood dreams are simply "not us." They never will be "us."

Choosing involves selection. Selection, by design, assumes the rejection of some things in favor of others. There is no selection without rejection. To choose is to embrace a particular option and to reject some—or many—other options. The natural next step in the movement to adulthood comes when the seeker/dreamer begins to decide what she wants to be—and what she doesn't want to be. Some young people make such decisions quickly. Others struggle with their choices for a while. But every healthy adult someday "tames" his or her dreams.

This step of the journey causes some anxiety and grief, but it can also bring peace of mind. The anxiety that attends such decision-making has a lot to do with the lack of confidence we feel at making any important choice: "Have I made the right decision?" "Did I ignore another possibility?" "Will this choice eliminate my options?" "Is there a better choice I haven't seen yet?" Anxiety during such times of "letting go" is normal, for it reflects the fear that setting aside an option closes a door of opportunity permanently. Sometimes that is the case—but not always. We may also fear that in eliminating an option, we could be denying a voice to a portion of ourselves—perhaps a talent that may go unexplored when a door is closed.

The grief that attends such self-definition comes from giving up a dream about ourselves we may have lived with for a long time. If our identity was connected to a hope or dream we are dismissing, we feel that we are losing a part of ourselves by relinquishing that dream. Letting go of a given choice may mean closing the door to some highly valued expectations and fantasies. Reducing our options could imply rejection of a piece of the puzzle we prized as "me." Or the dream may have been a long-held expectation a family member had for us, and we don't want to hurt that individual. Growing up often means giving up some fantasies that were never meant to be. We grieve the death of dreams and fantasies—unrealistic though they may have been. Adulthood is sometimes a stark invitation into reality.

Hence the act of choosing or deciding contributes an important element to the "recipe" of adulthood. Each of us may experiment and investigate for a while. The act of choosing gives boundary and definition to our journey and thus offers a significant closure to the open-ended "trip of discoveries" from youth to adulthood.

If on the one hand these acts of choosing evoke anxiety and grief, then on the other hand they provide security and focus. When we begin to declare choices along the way, the unclear content of who we are and what we are going to do gains a dimension of specificity. In choosing, we find focus and lose a dimension of the uncertainty in our lives. To choose is to own certain decisions, and the clarity choosing provides brings security to the journey we've undertaken.

Choosing (deciding) brings a new dimension to our personal growth: the gift of commitment. Tentativeness and uncertainty have their place on the road to personal definition. Maturity, on the other hand, offers us the valuable gifts of responsibility and reliability. To own the capacity to affirm a certain choice, commit to a specific dream, or become faithful to a particular belief, cause, or job is to exercise our power of *fidelity*. Made in the image of God, each of us carries the capacity to act in ways that emulate the character of the divine. One of the most significant characteristics of God we possess is the capacity to make commitments and keep them. The God who gave life to Adam, Noah, Abraham, Isaac, and Jacob is a God who made covenants with these persons. Such promises reflect an individual's capacity to commit to a certain point of view and to remain faithful to it. Choosing and deciding as we describe it is no other than the God-given ability to commit ourselves to certain enterprises, and by such promises to remain true to those choices with determination and continuity. Such capacities are often identified as "character" in an individual.

Choosing or deciding a certain course of action need not be for a lifetime. Some of the choices we make are for a given period of time. Responsible and reliable commitments have different forms and timetables. What distinguishes what we say or do in this part of the journey is that at this juncture in life, we are prepared to stand by what we decide—for the period of time or the way in which we declared that we would do so. Identity and vocation, as we have mentioned before, may have multiple dimensions and choices. The distinguishing characteristic we offer in this part of the journey is that we assume responsibility and become reliable in regard to promises and actions. We commit to certain choices because we will only discover a deeper dimension to ourselves and to our vocation by taking on a higher level of personal investment.

The Bible called such reliable promises "covenants." God sought to enter such commitments with a variety of human beings and hoped that they would respond with the same level of faithfulness. Fidelity to certain commitments is not intended to deprive us of any freedoms or confine us to fewer options. Rather, such faithfulness ushers us into a higher and deeper dimension of purpose and personal investment, rewarding us with deeper fulfillment ("The thief cometh but to steal, and to kill, and to destroy; I have come that they might have life, and that they have it more abundantly" [John 10:10, KJV]).

The movement toward adulthood includes a journey through dreaming and imagining, seeking and searching, striving and wrestling, and choosing and deciding. Along the journey, several distracting myths interfere with a young person's progress. We shall next identify some of those myths, challenge their accuracy, and learn how to move beyond them so that adulthood may be found with the minimum amount of confusion and frustration.

Section 2

Common
Myths on the
Road to
Adulthood

Several myths distract and distress young people as they take the trip from late adolescence to adulthood. Some of these untruths have been handed down from generation to generation without ever being questioned. Some of the assumptions we challenge have been taught and maintained in the local church. A few of them have come from people we've admired as role models along the way. Many of these half-truths are beliefs held by the society and community in which we grew up. We identify them here to enable today's young pilgrims to resist their message, to examine the truth some myths ignore, and to move beyond them to maturity and truth. "If you continue in my word, then you shall know the truth, and the truth shall set you free" (John 8:31-32, KJV).

Myth #1: Spending Time on Myself Is Selfish

One of the recurring messages in Christian communities is that believers are expected to focus on others, not themselves. Appropriate and true as the message is, it often is not understood in the context of personal development. All human beings need to spend time understanding themselves *in order to* know how to serve and minister to others. We need to know enough about ourselves and what we believe before we can effectively care and be cared for. Focusing on other people requires a maturity that only comes with personal awareness and perspective. Christ himself declared that believers ought to love others as they love themselves. The Master himself spent time (from ages twelve to thirty?) preparing himself for service—and even after his baptism spent quite a long time in the desert rehearsing his priorities. We rarely mention that "forty days and forty nights" in the desert meant "a very long time" and that the questions expressed during the temptations had to do with who he was, how he was using his gifts, and what his primary purposes were (check the three questions mentioned in the Gospel accounts of the temptations of Christ).

Young people are often made to feel guilty for spending time on themselves. How else can a person discover who they are and what they find important? The questions Jesus Christ was asking, even during the temple visit at age twelve, had to do with what he was learning about himself, what he believed, and how he was to live. There is no substitute for the "homework" of self-discovery.

Late adolescents and young adults need to spend time thinking about themselves in order to dream and imagine a self. Self-focus at their age is not only desirable, but necessary. The emerging adult is at this point just beginning the important task of differentiating herself from her family of origin. The habits and behaviors of family members are being scrutinized in relationship to what the young person knows about himself, and an individual's capacity to do such mental evaluation is crucial for maturation. Often called "critical thinking" by students of human development, such reflections are important mental exercises. Self-focus is an essential first ingredient in "separating" a young person's thoughts and feelings from the pool of thoughts and feelings the family has provided. In the absence of such personal reflection, a person has no sense of himself as a separate individual, uniquely made as no other person, in the image of God.

If ever in the cycle of development a person should be encouraged to become self-absorbed, that time is late adolescence. Critical as we are of adults who never move beyond self-absorption, we should not confuse the emotional immaturity of adult self-absorption with the hard work that young people do in their reverie, self-concern, and auto-focus. How else can they learn who they are?

Again, the useful self-preoccupation of late adolescence and young adulthood needs to be tempered so that it neither becomes obsessive nor paralyzing. Worrying about oneself is neither constructive nor appropriate. An excessive self-preoccupation can become debilitating. Self-interest can soon become inappropriate self-service—even in youth. Self-absorption becomes debilitating when an individual spends excessive amounts of time reflecting on herself. Self-focus needs to find balance in activities and projects that take individuals away from themselves, so that they don't spend time only on themselves. Again, self-preoccupation becomes debilitating when an individual focuses mainly on the negative aspects of life. Young people tend to be hyper self-critical anyway, and added hours of negative "self-talk" usually lead to dejection or depression.

Churches and other institutions can contribute to positive experiences in self-reflection by helping young people understand the spiritual role self-focus plays in personal development and spiritual formation. Youth groups and leaders of young people can spend more time educating teenagers on the appropriate and valuable use of personal reverie for spiritual growth. Religious groups where young people can safely share their dreams and reflections will contribute to the biblical injunction of "training up a child in their own particular way" (Prov 22:6) so that they may grow into the fullness of God's purpose for them (Luke 2:40). Communities of faith can help individuals by providing them with perspective in self-assessment and by keeping them from isolating themselves in their own reflection.

Myth #2: Most of My Needs Are Unimportant

I still remember the mother's comment to a friend about her four-year-old daughter's behavior: "Oh, ignore her; she's just wanting attention." Children *and* adults have legitimate needs. Our challenge has usually been to express those needs in appropriate ways. Here is a list of some of the needs human beings possess, none of which we outgrow:

1. The need for attention: the gift of someone's presence and interest
2. The need for acceptance: to be forgiven and received as we are
3. The need for appreciation: to be valued individually
4. The need for encouragement: the importance of being strengthened
5. The need for support: to be nurtured or fed emotionally, physically, and spiritually
6. The need for affection: our need for physical and emotional intimacy
7. The need for security: to feel safe
8. The need for respect: to be recognized/validated as worthy
9. The need for consistency: to rely on the predictability and constancy of some things
10. The need for challenge: To aspire to new goals, capacities, standards
11. The need to create: To make something ourselves; to contribute in a unique way

Each of us has developed over time some means of identifying and meeting our needs—even if inadequate. Several issues contribute to having those needs met, and a few suggestions here may dispel some of the myths commonly associated with "outgrowing childish needs."

First of all, it is important to identify many of our needs as appropriate to every age. The list of needs mentioned above is not exhaustive, but a reader may be surprised to view them all as legitimate adult needs. Some people come from a family circle that minimized the importance of particular needs. Some appropriate needs are often ignored because they are not recognized. The list above should prove useful for identifying significance human needs and their relationship to a healthy sense of self—and therefore to a healthy personal identity.

Made in the image of God, every human deserves—and needs—some *attention*. We exist, by design, for relationships. God chose to make us so that God could enter a meaningful dialogue with other beings (Gen 1). Every relationship deserves some attention—some recognition. Even God wants some attention and invites human beings into a relationship precisely for such. The gift of someone's attention bestows upon a human being a sense of value and utility in life.

Every relationship requires awareness of (attention to) someone else. Martin Buber, one of the great Jewish theologians of the past century, identified this truth in an incisive book called *I and Thou*, in which he underscored the biblical concept that everyone exists in and for relationships. Buber affirmed that unless there was another being with whom to relate (a "thou"), there was no genuine experience of an "I." One of the necessary ingredients in human interaction is the gift of time and focus that one person gives another—attention. We all need "tending to" periodically.

Each of us also needs personal *acceptance*. We need to be received as a unique creation, fallible and fragile as we are. To know that we are accepted by someone else means that we "pass" as a human being. Late adolescents yearn for confirmation that they are acceptable—liked—even when they struggle to accept themselves. We also need reassurance that we are forgiven in relationships, so that we are not alienated from or rejected by those we love the most.

The need for *appreciation* taps our struggle to accept our own worth. Each human being wants to know that he or she is valued. We all need confirming evidence that we contribute to someone else's life and that someone else attaches worth to our existence. Appreciation is not a luxury; we feed on such acknowledgment for a sense of a believing in ourselves as worthwhile.

Encouragement and *support* are additional nutrients in the journey toward adulthood. The word "encourage" is derived from the French and Latin and contains the word "cour," which means "heart." To be encouraged is to be *given heart.* In order for a person to develop, he must continue his journey of discovery. Support and encouragement provide strength and endurance during the hard exercise of exploration of choices and the investigation of abilities. Without support and encouragement, most of us would leave the often difficult road of self-discovery. We need courage and nurture to survive challenges and failures in life.

Affection is another necessary ingredient for human survival. Studies with a variety of mammals and human beings confirm that the absence of physical expression renders infant offspring listless and unresponsive to normal behaviors. The biblical evidence in support of physical touch as a healing dynamic is obvious. "Medicine men" and healers from a variety of cultures and generations testify to the restorative powers of physical touch. The inappropriate and destructive use of touch has sometimes rendered physical contact suspicious, when in reality the appropriate contribution of affection to the benefit of the body, mind, and soul is immense.

Small children and adults alike attest to the importance of *security* in life. From the moment of birth—and even in the womb—human beings share the need for protection, safety, and the avoidance of injury. Beyond childhood and adolescence, every human being seeks physical, emotional, and spiritual safety. Vulnerable and fragile as the human creature is, each of us has appropriate needs for self-protection and self-preservation.

As subtle as the need may seem, we also want to be *respected.* Comedian Rodney Dangerfield made a living off the amusing comment, "I don't get no respect." One of the significant responses we can make to other human beings is the blessing of offering them respect. The communication of respect in any human interchange bestows upon the recipient a sense of being esteemed. Children learn to respect adults, and one of the most important affirmations a person can receive from another human being is the communication that they are held in high regard.

Consistency contributes a measure of reliability to our world. Change is constant. We also hope that some particular things remain constant. The reliability of certain boundaries, rules, and laws contributes a sense of continuity to the human spirit. The night's sleep is supposed to bring rest to the tired body. The ingestion of food assumes that the sensation of hunger will diminish. The morning sun heralds a brand new day—every day. Summer is hotter than winter. After winter, spring will arrive. Children and adolescents expect that their parents will take care of them until they have grown. We all need some predictability in our lives.

In order to grow, every creature needs *challenge.* Human development depends on the capacity to move beyond the border of yesterday's growth. The human spirit also responds strongly to a higher standard, a harder try, a longer reach, a greater strength.

Personal development depends on challenges to grow. Along with attraction to an added dimension, challenges cause people to move toward their full potential. Challenge is an appropriate need in every stage of our lives.

Made in the image of God, each of us also possesses a need to *create*. Like the God who made us, we thrive on the capacity to bring something into existence. To create is a need that seeks expression throughout adulthood. There are many ways to create, just as there are many human talents. Vocation and service give us many outlets through which to make something new.

Myth #3: Looking into the Past Is Useless

One of the common mistakes people make is that of dwelling excessively on the past or getting stuck trying to undo it. While neither of those exercises is healthy, "looking back" can be a useful way of freeing ourselves of unnecessary baggage on the road to adulthood. Such an exercise, properly undertaken, also gives people an opportunity to make conscious and personal choices about who they are and what they plan to do in life.

To ignore the recorded history of events and impressions stored over the years in our minds is to remain controlled by their unexamined influence. Experiences lodged in our brains are connected to emotional impressions and reactions. In order to free ourselves from their unconscious effects on choices and behaviors in our present and future, we need to examine their content and power.

Each of us carries emotional baggage containing particular memories and impressions. Some of those remembrances are pleasant, and some are traumatic. Some events are distorted by circumstance and time. Many of our habits, preferences, and prejudices were shaped by experiences in the past. The families we grew up in also influenced us with their preferences, biases, and habits. Identifying some of those "scripts" we learned from significant people in our life can help us decide how those beliefs and behaviors developed and whether we want to maintain them or discard them.

Looking into the past need not be disturbing or distasteful. Adolescents begin this examination in the process of noticing attitudes, thoughts, and behaviors in the families with whom they live. About the time they move away (physically or emotionally) from their family of origin, young adults often question some of these borrowed beliefs and inherited values. Identifying family scripts and roles is a helpful exercise in the journey of owning our own beliefs and behaviors. The capacity to distinguish between our own thoughts and perceptions and those of our parents is a critical step in the movement toward self-definition and personal identity formation.

When an individual decides to identify and evaluate some of the messages and attitudes that have shaped his life, he often chooses a familiar history-gathering device called a "genogram," which is an interview exercise in which one talks with various family members about family stories, history, and memories. This collection of information gives rise to a paper-drawn diagram that describes how various members of the family are connected over several generations. Informative as the interviews are, they also provide rich insight into how that family has thought, believed, and acted over a span of years. Such understanding offers the interviewer a clearer view of the values and choices that have shaped her past. In addition, the gathered picture offers the young adult an opportunity to choose her own set of values, issues, causes, and actions. Such choosing frees the seeker to establish her own identity and to take responsibility for her own decisions and preferences.

An examination of yesterday's history in our family can also provide insight into negative messages that have shaped either our own identity or that of the family. A recent example of such a personal study into his past led a young man to identify an inaccurate and paralyzing label of "quitters" that had plagued more than four generations of his family. Aware of the effect of that message in his own life, this young adult decided to challenge the destructive script and rewrite his own personal journal as that of a determined "finisher."

In such examinations, we may also discover that we have taken too much responsibility for an event in the past, or that we are still punishing ourselves for choices made years ago that need not shape our entire future. Looking into the past, then, can provide us a liberating personal experience of defining ourselves as an adult—of "becoming our own person," as the saying goes.

Myth #4: Setting Boundaries with Loved Ones Is Cold and Unloving

Somewhere along the way, some believers have confused the concept of unconditional love with the idea that love sets no boundaries. The same Messiah who declared to Peter—and to all disciples—that grace was to be extended seventy times seven in relationships also instructed his followers to "let the dead bury the dead" and leave their occupations to follow him. Christ himself declared limits to his relationships with his own family (Mark 3:31ff) and set boundaries to Peter's recommendations about the choices Christ should make (Matt 16:22). Requests made by trusted disciples (James and John) could not be granted if they interfered with the mission of the Messiah (Matt 20: 20-26).

If we set no boundaries in our relationships with others, they will assume control of our lives and time. Every person is to be respected as an individual, and each has the right to his or her own space, choices, and opinions. However, unless we set limits on what others demand of us, we have no separate self, and our purposes and thoughts do not matter.

What appears "cold" to us or others is that some of the boundaries we set hurt other people's feelings. One important distinction needs to be made in order to challenge this myth: there is an important difference between *hurting* someone and *harming* them. The culture in which we live often confuses the two. We may hurt someone's feelings by setting boundaries to their influence over us, but we may be helping them in the process rather than harming them. When Christ declared that he was to follow God's bidding over his family's wishes, he may have hurt their feelings temporarily, but he was not harming them. Harm would have come if he had followed what his mother and brothers wanted him to do (go home)—and ignored what God wanted him to do (launch his ministry). Family members may have felt rejected or may have struggled with their need to control him, but that was *their* issue, not his. When Jesus told a rich young ruler that he must give up his idolatry of things to follow Christ, he probably hurt his feelings, but he did him no harm (Mark 10: 17-22). Harm would have come if Jesus had pretended that the man had no problem and if he had only flattered him by saying something nice (which we often do in relationships, confusing hurting with harming!).

We can *do harm by not helping people in places where they need self-evaluation.* In counseling sessions I can do much harm by allowing individuals to maintain destructive patterns, never helping them to struggle with what they need to change in order to grow. In telling people what they need to hear, we may believe we have hurt them. The pain we see is usually the discomfort they are feeling for having to look at themselves or take responsibility for harmful behaviors. They may also hurt because of having to discontinue actions that have given them some degree of comfort or pleasure, even though they were harmful.

People who study families often talk about family members whose identity and self is *fused* with other members of the family. Such a term is used to describe relationships in which there are no boundaries or in which the boundaries are so unclear that the people involved have no sense of being a separate self. The reason we sometimes have to leave a family geographically or emotionally is that some families (or persons) give us little permission to think, feel, or act in a manner distinct from them. One of the important evaluations in late adolescence is to determine whether the family we grew up with gave us enough space to become a person in our own right. Each of us needs enough separation from others to have a distinct self. Created in the image of God, we are each unique beings, unlike anyone else. Setting boundaries helps achieve such clarity.

Setting boundaries in relationships, therefore, is not a negative action, but a gift to *both* persons in a relationship. When my son declares that he thinks or feels differently than I do, he both declares that he has his own identity and thoughts and that he respects me as a person who also has a separate and unique self as well. Boundaries protect and affirm both people in a relationship.

Can boundaries ever become harmful or "cold"? Certainly. The motivation behind the setting of boundaries has a lot to do with whether such separations are good or destructive. If we set boundaries primarily to punish another person in a relationship, that is harmful. If we set boundaries arbitrarily in order to reject someone or to distance ourselves from them mainly for the pleasure of seeing them hurt, we are using boundaries in an abusive or destructive way. The Sadducees and Pharisees sometimes created boundaries from Jesus that were actually *barriers* to understanding or dialogue (Luke 5:21, 30; 6:2).

In addition, some people are more sensitive to "invasion of privacy" than others, especially if others have subjected them to infringement. If we are regularly around persons who encroach on our boundaries and ignore our thoughts and feelings, we may become protective of our "territory" and react by creating more distance or responding anxiously to unclear boundaries. Setting boundaries in such relationships is an affirmation by the person that he or she is made in the image of God and deserves the respect of a personal opinion and thought. Distancing, then, is an attempt to define a self and a positive behavior in the pursuit of an adequate sense of selfhood.

Boundaries, in fact, provide us opportunities for discernment and self-evaluation so that we may grace another person with our own individuality. We all need some "mental space" in which to operate, and separation and limits offer us the private territory where we can distinguish our own voices and learn to share them with others.

Finally, the creation of boundaries enables us to separate our issues—and responsibilities—from others. Loved ones sometimes ask us to take responsibility for choices and actions that are not ours to do, but theirs. Folks may try to make us responsible for their work, their happiness (or their misery), or may want us to expend most of the effort in a relationship. We are not to do for others what they can do themselves. We actually cheat someone else of the privilege and responsibility of their choices and behaviors.

Myth #5: If I Have Faith, My Prayers Will Be Answered Immediately

Well-intentioned believers have inadvertently created this myth. It is a myth, first of all, because the Bible nowhere teaches that the speed of answered prayer is directly proportional to the depth of a petitioner's faith. Many a believer has become discouraged by the misperception that a delayed response to prayer is a reflection of one's poor spiritual condition. The methodical and often painstaking journey to adulthood is flooded with experiences that require both patience and time to flower into full purpose. When Abraham and Sarah were promised a child, the delayed fulfillment prompted an anxious Abraham to conceive Ishmael with a concubine (Gen 16). When Moses led the people of Israel to a promised land, the lengthy journey to it evoked complaint and impatience from the Israelites (Exod 16:2ff). The books of Joshua and Judges primarily describe a long and tedious conquest of a promised land that in fact never was fully conquered. The very promise of a Messiah is still an unfulfilled promise as far as most Jewish people are concerned, and it was a long-awaited appearance even for people of much faith (Joel 2:28; Hab 1:2; Zech 14:1ff, etc.). The birth of Christ was heralded for centuries, and a man of deep faith waited a lifetime to see it just before he died (Luke 2:25-32).

Christ's prayers were not always answered immediately either; many of his requests were for long-term issues and consequences (John 17; Matt 26:36-39). Paul, a servant of deep faith, asked for the removal of a thorn, and his never-granted request had nothing to do with lack of faith (2 Cor 12:7-9). Obviously, the speed of answered prayer has little to do with amount of faith. Christ him- self declared to the apostles that if they had faith the size of a mustard seed, they could do wonders (Luke 17: 5-6). Petitions and inquiries that relate to identity and vocation require time and experience as a response. Like the baking of a cake, some develop- ments cannot be rushed.

Other petitions in prayers are for immediate relief or speedy clarity. Sometimes we are not given answers to such petitions because the process of a measured and labored response is what we need for resolution. Therapists report that some amounts of anxi- ety and discomfort are the only "ingredients" that produce motivation for change and the determination to grow in people. Under duress, we may, then, often be praying for exactly the opposite of what we need. That is why Jesus in the garden of Gethsemane provides us a very useful model of petitionary prayer: having declared what relief he wanted and expressed the pain and dread he was feeling, he concluded the prayer by saying, "nevertheless, not as I will, but as thou wilt" (Matt 26:39, KJV).

Christ's closing comment in that prayer reminds us of one additional possibility. Sometimes we pray not only for things that require time, but we also request things that are not good for us. In our limited insight and hasty judgment, we often ask for things that will not help us and that must be refused. The wisdom of asking for God's will to be done is a an acknowledgment that God knows better what we need than we do—a comment Christ expressed caringly in the Sermon on the Mount (Matt 7:11). A heavenly parent knows much better than we do what gifts (petitions) are appropriate and inappropriate for us.

Myth #6: Doubt Is an Enemy to Faith

Doubt is, in fact, essential to the personal ownership of our faith. All of us grow up with a borrowed set of beliefs, and at certain points on the journey, we need to begin to examine those choices to determine if they reflect what *we* believe. If we fail to question our secondhand beliefs, they will be just that: secondhand, and therefore neither deeply felt, long lasting, nor personally espoused. When young people are beginning to doubt and are told not to doubt, the message we communicate is that our belief system— and theirs—is fragile enough that it cannot bear scrutiny. An essential part of the Jewish rite of passage into adulthood, celebrated as bar mitzvah, is the twelve- or thirteen-year-old male's visit to a temple or synagogue, at which time he may ask any question of the rabbis or question any aspects of his faith. Jesus himself participated in this ritual and astonished the doctors at the temple not because he was posing questions—every youth did—but because of the depth of his questions, his wisdom, and his tenacity (Luke 2:43-48). (Note that his parents missed him for three days!)

Doubting a long-held belief can throw us off balance and create anxiety. Adults and parents who respond defensively to the inquiring dialogue of a young person are usually confessing that they themselves have questioned little in their faith journey. They may be afraid of inquiring into their own faith and belief systems for fear of what they might discover about their spiritual pilgrimages. When I was a trustee at a Baptist university several years ago, a pastor in the state expressed concern that his own son "had lost his faith" studying in the Religion Department of the university. At first, few people in the room took notice that his comment was less a reflection of the department than a comment on the rigid and borrowed set of beliefs in which he had been brought up (I myself was a graduate of the same department). At the meeting, I responded, "My, it sounds like he came here with a pretty fragile set of personal beliefs, doesn't it, if one course in a college can wipe out all he affirmed."

Young people themselves can also become anxious about losing their faith. Disillusioned or discouraged by beliefs that don't seem to fit their current challenges, some young people conclude that their entire faith system is invalid. We can help them during such uncertain times, first, by remaining models of an unswerving set of convictions *we* espouse, giving them hope that their faith may also have a future. In the second place, we can also walk beside them in their quandaries and confusion without judging them or lecturing them, but instead listening carefully to their struggles and doubts. By doing so, we give them confidence that they will resolve their faith concerns and that we believe in their capacity to do so. In the third place, we may help them by reassuring them that solid convictions are built on strong foundations and that their questioning and doubting contribute to a personalized and firsthand internalizing of their faith. We may even underscore the validity of a belief system forged in a gradual and growing journey of faith.

Rather than an atmosphere of fear and suspicion when questions are raised, churches and families need to provide youth with a platform at home and in the congregation where inquiry and evaluation can be taken seriously and every question examined openly without timidity. Such an environment was the one in which Jesus Christ grew up. The dialogue and care that such an attitude evokes is one of trust, interest, and deeper faith. In such an environment, young people can learn not only what kinds of questions are most productive for a vibrant faith, but they can also learn (with much more confidence) to question their doubts! As any serious student of human behavior can verify, an atmosphere of honest and open inquiry breeds a healthy and mature faith, for whenever some questions cannot be asked or some topics never discussed, a perception about their "power" is created. Folks who think they are strengthening faith by discouraging or punishing inquiry are doing exactly the opposite: they are telling inquirers that their own faith is not strong enough to withstand scrutiny. Like the children of Israel, captives in a foreign land (Babylon) and dependent on a "safe faith" that never faced difficulty, young people need the privilege of investigation and evaluation of their faith to see if it is a "traveling faith." In captivity, many Israelites had a faith that wouldn't survive into adulthood, and they couldn't sing the songs of Zion without their childhood trappings (Ps 137: 1ff)

Myth #7: Other People Are Responsible for My Behavior

No doubt the family that nurtured us taught us most of our behaviors. In addition, our childhood environment, the church we attended, our location, and our many experiences have all contributed to the way we think, feel, and act. But none of the above persons or experiences are responsible for our thoughts, feelings, and actions. *We* are responsible for our thoughts, feelings, choices, and actions. As chaplain to a women's prison in Kentucky for several years, one of my responsibilities was to teach the resident inmates how to develop self-control and take responsibility for their own choices and behaviors. Most of them struggled with the myth, so common in our society, that other people are responsible (or to blame) for our actions, feelings, and thoughts. Some of the folks in that penitentiary had difficulty grasping this concept. They wanted to believe that someone else was responsible for the way they thought or acted.

Most of us are captive to that same myth. While we have learned certain ways of thinking and responded with feelings and actions as a consequence of being taught by others, no one else is responsible for our thoughts or can create our thoughts. Part of growing up involves a transition from childhood ways of thinking to adult ways of thinking and acting. Children employ concrete or literal thinking, a way of understanding that cannot comprehend symbols or analogies. Abstract, symbolic thinking allows us to separate our thoughts, feelings, and behaviors from those of others, to use "as if" analogies, and to compare different realities without making unwarranted connections between them. These unwarranted connections are sometimes called "magical thinking," and they develop in childhood when our brain connections "glue" events and thoughts together—whether they belong together or not. The child angry with his father over yesterday's issue, on hearing today that his father had a car accident on his way home, fears that his negative feelings toward Dad may have caused it. The little girl whose parents divorce may believe *she* is the cause of their separation because she heard them arguing about her.

Magical thinking is not confined to children. The adolescent who sees the girl who just rejected his request for a date turn to a girlfriend and laugh about a joke concludes that the two girls are making fun of *him*. The explanation that a teenager gives to an inappropriate or illegal behavior in the company of peers: "It's *their* fault. They made me do it." Or the lonely young adult sits at home, isolated, and declares, "Nobody likes me. No one wants to be my friend, or they would call me." Magical thinking is basically connecting two unrelated events—or connecting a thought to an unrelated or coincidental occurrence. When we blink our eyes and the electricity is interrupted in our house, that doesn't mean the blinking of our eyes caused the interruption in the electric power. Hopefully, as adults, we've figured out that those two events were simultaneous but unconnected—accidental.

The reality, however, is that most of us regularly make assumptions that two unrelated experiences are connected, and we believe those assumptions without question! We blame chairs for getting in our way when we trip, as if they could actually move. We get angry when someone says something we don't like and say, "You made me angry," as if they were responsible for creating *our* feelings. We become anxious about a decision and jump to a conclusion (to relieve the stress we feel), but then say, "You rushed me, or I wouldn't have done it." We may also keep blaming our past on our current thoughts, feelings, and behaviors. It is essential that we begin to take responsibility for each of those as *ours* now because we have the power to control how we think, claim our own feelings, and control and choose our own behaviors. Taking this next step in assuming personal responsibility for who we are and how we function is a key element in becoming an adult.

A word to the wise: Just because people reach adulthood chronologically doesn't mean they have decided to take responsibility for their thoughts, feelings, or actions. Many adults still live with the myth that someone else is responsible for their behavior or their feelings. They remain captive to the lie that they have no control over their lives. They have thus surrendered their present and their future to the myth that other people are both in charge of them and to blame for how they choose, think, feel, or act. Such folks usually fool themselves into believing that other people are also responsible for whether they themselves are happy or not. (No one else is responsible for our happiness!)

Myth #8: Everybody Knows What They Want to Do in Life but Me

To listen to people talk, we might think they are all quite sure about what they want to do in life. That perception is not true. More than 50 percent of college graduates are doing something totally unrelated to their college majors within a year of graduation. Most young people join the military because they don't know what they want to do for a living and want to buy time and perhaps earn cash. As we visit with non-college-bound high school graduates and dropouts, we learn from them that they mostly "fell into" their jobs. They tell us that they didn't want to go to school anymore, that they had no idea what to study if they went to school, that they were ready to be on their own financially, or that they had to work because their family expected them or needed them to do so.

Most young people and adults make a vocational decision every five to seven years. Sometimes we don't discuss the decision openly or raise the issue directly, but we do revisit our vocational options rather frequently. Pressure from family and friends often prompts a quick and clear response about what we're doing or planning to do in regard to the future and employment, but deep inside of us, the certainty of our answers gives way to the doubt and confusion we actually feel about what we are doing—or think of doing.

Some people have grown up in church confusing the "narrow road" with their vocational choices. There are scores of persons who actually believe they only have the talent or skill for *one* vocation and that their failure to find that one perfect job will cause them much displeasure. Granted, vocational choices today are often connected to costly educational pursuits. No doubt some of us feel that once we have chosen a vocation, others will judge us as irresponsible if we don't stick with it. And some young people prefer the safety of staying with the job they have rather than experimenting with a new and untried path. But whether we publicize our vocational struggles or not, the fact of the matter is that most of us spend a lot of energy and time sorting out the business of our skills and chosen vocations—for quite some time.

The more useful question for us to ask during the early years of adulthood is "What's the first vocation I want to try with the skills I have?" This leads us to myth #9.

Myth #9: There Is Only One Vocation God Has Equipped Me to Do

The twenty-first-century adult will change primary vocations four times in a span of forty-five years. Since the average lifespan exceeds eighty years, most of us will probably try at least that many vocations! No doubt there are many people we know who have stayed in one vocation all their lives. Just a few years ago, folks felt fortunate to experience *one* job. That reality, however, says nothing about their untried abilities and unexplored skills. As we mentioned before, there are many reasons people stick to one particular job or another: (1) the time and cost of training for a different vocation is prohibitive; (2) the risks of changing and transitioning to another kind of work are often high; (3) the security of the job we know may make it too attractive to leave; (4) the fear that we have no adequate skills for a different job may hinder us; and (5) the loyalty we feel toward a certain institution or its people may overrule our desire to try a different calling.

The mistaken impression that God has equipped us for only one kind of work may also keep us from exploring our options. Most of our vocational models in the Bible were persons with multiple vocations, yet we tend to see them in only one dimension or role. Jacob was a cook, a tender of sheep, and eventually a businessman. Joseph was a sheepherder, a house servant, and an administrator. Moses was a prince, a nomad, a sheepherder, and a prophet. David was a sheepherder, a musician, a soldier, and a king. Paul was a tent maker, a preacher, a missionary, and a writer. God has equipped us with far more skills than we will ever use in a lifetime. God shares the abundance of creation by giving us more talents than we will ever use but also by giving us the opportunity to choose which ones we use during our lifetime. We were never meant to use all our skills; at the banquet table of God's gifts to us, there has always been more than enough. The adventure to which we were invited is to take ourselves seriously enough to discover which gifts suit us best and will be most worthy of our efforts.

No doubt today's expensive cost of vocational training has discouraged vocational pursuits. Sincere efforts at choosing a path for the future place some of us in the uncomfortable position of appearing immature or unstable if we suggest a career change midstream. We also fear that vocational changes will label as wasted the time and money expended earlier on a vocation. Yet in the economy of God's evolving gifts, most of us who have engaged in several vocations have discovered that each training, study, and experience builds upon the last one, so that the skills we learn in one vocational chapter contribute to the next ones. Moses, for example, had the opportunity to study in Egypt as only a prince was allowed. His flight to the desert gave him a chance to learn the patience required not only to tend sheep, but to lead a wandering, disorganized, sometimes frightened people across a desert. His wrenching displacement from Egypt into a foreign territory also equipped him to understand the mind and heart of a homeless, nomadic, and frightened people caught between a troubled past and a distant and unclear hope. Each chapter in his life contributed to the breadth and wisdom of the leader Israel needed to oversee the perilous journey to the promised land. Each vocation and job informs the next labor. There is no waste in the investigation of many skills. They are the notes that form the song waiting to be composed individually in each person's heart.

Myth #10: If People Really Knew Me, They Wouldn't Like Me

Eric Berne decades ago introduced the insight that most people think others are superior to themselves. In an challenging book titled *I'm Okay, You're Okay* (New York: Harper & Row, 1969). Berne suggested that human beings adopt one of four postures in life that determine how they see themselves and others. We can see ourselves as adequate or capable (OK), or we may see ourselves as inferior and ill equipped compared to others (Not OK). We also see others as capable and adequate (OK), or the opposite (Not OK). A psychiatrist, Berne discovered in his practice that a majority of human beings secretly judge others as better, more adequate, more capable, more liked, etc., than themselves. He described this posture as "I'm Not Okay, You're Okay," and suggested that most persons adopt this outlook in relationships.

Berne was not intimating that such persons were correct in their judgment of themselves and others. He was describing the curious (and unfortunate) truth that many people *assume* that their friends and neighbors are all superior to themselves—and that others are better liked than themselves. Berne's interpretation identified the same myth that Virginia Satir once described as one of our family or individual "secrets" (*Conjoint Family Therapy* [Behavior Science Books, 1964]). In the private compartments of our lives, all of us have secret fears, and one prevailing fear is that we are inadequate compared to others. Our private view of ourselves is so negative that we believe if other people knew us they would not like us. Apparently, many of us live with the suspicion that if the truth were told about us, our friends and neighbors would reject us.

The sad effect of this misperception is that we live as if this lie were true. We tell ourselves that we are more poorly equipped than other people. We feel inferior to others. We think others are more "together" than we are. The reality is that our "secret self" is not really that bad, and we are actually neither inferior nor worse than anyone else. Under such negative judgments, our failures and secrets quickly get out of proportion and loom larger than they really are. Meanwhile, our superficial perception of others often renders them as doing much better than we are.

One of the important contributions of small groups structured with levels of trust, truth, and care is that they provide a far more accurate picture of ourselves and how other people see us. People who know us better actually like us better. People who exchange "secrets" in care and trust discover a commonality that brings them together, not apart. Sharing our fallibility and fears bring us grace and acceptance from others, not rejection. Since every human being is fallible, the discovery of that imperfection actually fosters a mutuality of forgiveness and support that bonds people together rather than separating them. Such developments in small groups are what the church as an organism was designed to provide its members. Unfortunately, such positive experiences occur too rarely in a local congregation, where "emotional distance" is employed for personal safety, competition fosters envy, and betrayal of secrets breeds pain and fear rather than compassion and grace.

The truth behind this myth probably sounds like this: "If some people really knew me as I know myself, they would judge me and reject me as harshly as I treat myself. Others would accept me and love me as a person like themselves, fallible and unfinished, and worthy of a safe relationship." The majority of people who get to know us will like us; a few of those persons will actually like us *very much*!

Myth #11: My Friends Are Happier with Themselves than I Am

Carl Jung, a veteran student of human personality, talked about a "created image" of ourselves that he called a *persona* (Carl G. Jung, *Modern Man in Search of A Soul* [Orlando: Harcourt, 1935]). Often a product of the society in which we live, the persona is an artificial, outward perception of who we really are. Most of us play certain roles in public, acting out certain behaviors that "mask" our true feelings and thoughts. This created persona we show others is rarely our true self, for, as we just mentioned, we try to hide who we think we are from others for fear of rejection, misunderstanding, or embarrassment.

We live in a society that "masks" its true feelings constantly. The outward appearance of persons we see on a daily basis camouflages their thoughts and feelings enough that we rarely know what they are really like. Even our friends and close associates are "posturing" around us, making it difficult for us to ascertain what they actually think and feel. It is therefore unlikely that we know how content or happy most people are. If people in general were honest, however, they would confess to a general feeling of unease with themselves and the lives they lead. A careful exercise of listening to how others talk about who they are and what they are doing will reveal a repeated message of cautious concern.

The truth, again, is that the people we know are far more like us than a contrast to us. We are all explorers in an unknown land, searching somewhat anxiously for an unfound focus and passion that will bring lasting satisfaction. We are restless and impatient to find it, often because we erroneously believe that everyone else has already found it and we're late.

Happiness itself is a strange notion. Its root word derives from the concept "to happen," which suggests that it is an occurrence over which we have no control. Joy, by contrast, is a concept described in the Bible as an inner disposition over which we have control. Joy, as opposed to happiness, has mostly to do with how we see and interpret life *from within*. Unlike an experience exterior to myself that brings me a certain feeling, joy develops as an inner disposition based upon how I view and respond to life. Early Christians were often tortured and persecuted for their faith. As Paul described, they retained their capacity for joy on the basis of their inner attitude regardless of outward circumstances. We cannot control what happens to us; we can only control how we respond to whatever occurs. Happiness occurs at random, by accident. Joy, by contrast, is a state of being.

Since joy depends only on our ability to see, interpret, and respond to events from within, regardless of outward circumstances, we have a lot to do with whether we are joyful. Joy is not the masking of reality, however; joy is taking charge of how we engage in and respond to all the circumstances in life—whether fair or unfair. Joy is a cultivated attitude that shapes how we respond to experiences in the world by paying attention to our thoughts and reactions. Most of our feelings are created by the thoughts we entertain. What we say to ourselves will have a lot to do with how we face each event in life. If we tell ourselves, "All my friends are adjusting to life better than I am" (a common myth), then we will probably feel anger, sadness, and despair. If, on the other hand, we tell ourselves, "Some of my friends are adjusting well, and others are struggling with issues like I am," we would more likely generate some positive feelings internally. If, even further, we told ourselves, "Almost all my friends have some struggles with life, and I am pleased for those few who don't," we probably would generate even more positive feelings.

Myth #12: If I Had Any Skills, They Would Have Shown Up by Now

Writer Gore Vidal, as we have mentioned, once remarked, "America suffers from the idolatry of the immediate and the superficial." Many of us are impatient, especially about our dreams and our futures. We want to know *now*. The idea of a developing sense of self and skills is rarely respected. Anxiety controls our journey. We are afraid that we will not find anything we like, that our peers are "ahead of us," or that "ordinary days" in our pursuit are wasteful. Even an expectant mother has to wait nine months for the development and birth of a life.

Skills don't show up immediately. Abilities don't surface all at the same time. Talents often lie dormant, waiting for the right combination of events to flourish. Several of our gifts are employable in a variety of vocations. The development of gifts runs parallel to the growth of muscles. Exercise and practice build us physiologically, and the same occurs in regard to our abilities. The more we practice and experiment, the clearer our skills and limitations will appear. The greater we employ and use our potential abilities, the better they will develop. We must give time and work to develop our skills. Like the regular practice of individual orchestra players, we must sometimes work individually on the honing of our gifts. We must also understand that different gifts come together at different times to form a growing harmony that becomes a symphony—after much practice.

Few worthwhile things come together or work immediately. The late teens and the twenties should be a time dedicated to the investigation, experimentation, and development of our skills. Yet, like the increased synchronicity of a track athlete gaining momentum with each practice, we have a lifetime of development to anticipate and enjoy. Most of our skills don't "peak" at thirty. The sad piece in the partial discovery of many of our talents is that we become discouraged over what we've found and abandon too soon the pursuit of a skill.

Myth #13: If I Know and Understand Something, It Will Change Me

Many people live with the misunderstanding that knowledge or information changes behavior. Actually, our capacity to resist

change often trumps our desire to improve or grow. Just because I
know or understand some new insight doesn't mean that I will
choose to behave in a different way. One of our common myths is
that something is learned when we have knowledge of it or understand it. I know a scientist recently retired in Baltimore who has
spent years researching the behavior patterns of various mammals.
He shared with me several years ago that he and his colleagues
were impressed with the learning curve of human beings: "Dan,
human beings are probably the only mammals we know that learn
a way of doing something that doesn't work—and then do it over
and over again." Apparently even mice change their behavior in
the face of failure, frustration, or new information. We human
beings, however, tend to repeat behaviors that we know won't
work, hoping by increased intensity or repetition to reverse our
poor results.

When I was chaplain at the women's prison in Kentucky, one
of my responsibilities was to teach the residents principles of
behavior modification in order to help them with anger management and behavior control issues. Working in small groups and
presentations, I used instruction, illustration, and dialogue under
supervision of psychiatrists to communicate "Rational Behavior
Therapy" (RBT), in which I explained to women who had learned
to react to certain words by fighting that their response was a poor
learned reaction they had adopted over several years. I emphasized
that they could "relearn" that they didn't have to punch somebody
who directed profanity toward them or insulted their families. The
women understood what I was teaching them and agreed that
their chosen behavior was both learned and self-defeating. But
when facing the possibility of parole within weeks, most of them
could be "suckered" into a fight with another resident simply by

being called a name in the cafeteria or hallway. They lost a chance at parole because, even knowing better, they chose to react in learned ways that had gotten them in trouble before.

There is a price for changing and growing, and we often don't want to pay it. Simply knowing a "truth" does not mean we follow it. Knowing more about us has no magic changing effect upon us. We must *decide* to change or grow and commit ourselves to the chosen truth by transforming our thinking and behavior. Don Quixote de La Mancha, in Cervantes' enjoyable masterpiece, has the main character calling Aldonza, the common servant and street person, by the name Dulcinea, for he sees in her the better person and the higher standard others have missed. She resists his image of her, arguing that he does not see her for who she really is. At his death bed, she seeks him out to thank him for seeing her for who she could become, and declares that she has willed to become "Dulcinea." Change only occurs when thought and behavior are modified. There is no magic in knowledge that can transform us; we must choose to change by choosing to think and act in a new way.

That is why the Bible speaks of conversion (to reverse one's position or direction) as an issue of the heart, not simply the mind (2 Sam 7:21; 2 Chr 6:14; Isa 32:6; Jer 3:10; Matt 13:15; Luke 6:45, etc.). Conversion affects behavior, or it is not conversion (a new way of thinking and acting).

Myth #14: Everything That Happens Has a Purpose

One of the regular misguided "proverbs" in religious circles is that nothing happens by accident, or everything that happens has a "reason." The problem with such a well-intentioned point of view is that it leaves no room for chaos in the world, forgetting that this world is still not always under God's control and will ("Thy kingdom come, thy will be done . . ."). Random activity and free action is still at work. It is one thing to say everything that happens has potential to become purposeful, or to declare that God can *give* meaning and purpose to any event. But to declare that every occurrence in the world is initially purposeful is both deterministic and simplistic. In the Bible, God moved into the chaos (Gen 1) to give it form and purpose, and God continues to do so in this imperfect world. Still, the world is indeed imperfect and chaotic and not always subject to God's will. In addition, in the same Genesis chapter, God also gave human beings freedom to exercise their own will (Gen 1:27-28), which means that in this world God's will is not always done. That is precisely why we pray the words we pray in the Lord's prayer: as Christ taught us, we regularly ask that God's will and way enter this imperfect arena where it has not yet occurred.

To suggest that everything happens for a reason also damages the character of God, who must then be blamed for things you and I have done or choices you and I have made. It further ignores the reality reflected in Romans 8:21ff, in which Paul reminds us that the "whole creation groans in labor pains," still subject to futility and purposelessness. God is at work redeeming the entire created order (including us), but that redemptive work is not yet finished, and we, along with creation, are still not completely subject to God's perfect will. That is why earthquakes and hurricanes still besiege us; God can make good plans and purpose even from their chaotic work, but God did not create them.

The inmate who pounded on my door at the prison asking me why God had killed her husband —who died on his way to pick her up to go home—was doing what a number of people do. She was blaming God for choices human beings make because God gave us free will (in this husband's case, he exercised the free will of driving about ninety miles an hour down a narrow stretch of road). If we hold God responsible for everything that happens, we are both exonerating ourselves ("I am not to blame"), and at the same time *blaming God* for all kinds of mischief and destructive work. We've then even left out one of our other favorite other excuses: "The devil made me do it."

Challenging this myth means one certain thing: in giving us free will, God is also not responsible for our choices or our mistakes. That truth also underscores the reality that some of our choices are neither God's will nor God's work. No doubt God can insert purpose and redemption in any of our poor choices—God has been doing such since creation—but let's not blame God for choices *we* make or events still subject to the random caprice of an unredeemed creation.

Myth #15: If I'm Following God's Will, I Will Not Suffer

There is such a thing as unnecessary and unfair pain in this world, but not all suffering is bad. The notion that people who follow God's will are protected from physical suffering has no clear support in the Scriptures and has been the object of much misunderstanding (note Ps 91: 9-13, for example). When the Tempter uses this argument in the temptation dialogue (Matt 4:5-7) to lure Jesus , the Master quotes Deuteronomy 6:16 as a rebuttal, declaring that we should not test God's goodness (Exod 17:2 and Isa 7:12 allude to the same principle). Clearly, God's goodness is not to be tested by setting up potential physical dangers to see if God will intervene. That unfortunate misuse of God's care appears in the so-called "proof of faith" ceremonies where misguided believers have handled poisonous snakes in an attempt to confirm God's protection of them. The unique experience of Paul's survival after the bite of a viper (Acts 28) was not recorded as a recommended ritual to verify each believer's faith, but as a confirmation of God's care of Paul and his mission during a shipwreck and danger in his journey.

Followers in the Bible sometimes *did* believe that God would protect them from all harm, and they were deeply disappointed when such was not the case. The psalmist in Psalm 91:9-13 declares that God's faithful people will come to no physical, emotional, or spiritual harm. But that was never God's promise to the people of Israel, as confirmed in story after story of their history (read the accounts of the exodus, the conquest of the promised land, the exile, and the various occupations of Israel over the centuries). The book of Job also attests to the possibility of profound and prolonged suffering by the believer. Israelites eventually understood that God's promise to followers was for spiritual protection, not physical or emotional safety.

One of the parallel myths associated with this misunderstanding is the notion that life "will always be fair" for the follower. This naive misperception of our imperfect and capricious world does not take into account the myth #14. If God's will is not always done "on earth," then unfair and destructive events can occur all the time. God never promised that this world would be fair—only that God would be fair. Jesus Christ in Gethsemane and Golgotha faced the painful unfairness of this life; Paul lived with a thorn from which he got no relief. Job may have gotten his wealth back, but even a new wife and children didn't make up for the loss of the first family members.

One most important truth about suffering still remains to be stated. Some pain is unfair and pointless; but *not all suffering is pointless*. There is purpose and gift in some suffering. There are some important gains in life that cannot be attained without pain. We often speak of "growing pains" because there is a cluster of experiences that take on value only through the presence of suffering. The athlete who prepares to compete can only reach the measure of excellence desired by enduring the pain fitness requires. The parent who embraces the joy of loving a child must also suffer the mystery and struggle of that child's growth. The person who wants to grow emotionally must move through the pain of giving up childish ways. There are dimensions of suffering that create character. There is pain that brings about purpose and focus. Suffering also contributes strength and determination to a situation.

The Apostle Paul delineates some of his personal sufferings in 2 Corinthians 4:8-12: ". . . We are troubled on every side, yet not distressed; we are perplexed, but not in despair; persecuted, but not forsaken, cast down, but not destroyed; always bearing about in the body the dying of the Lord Jesus . . . ." The Apostle to the Gentiles was describing another dimension in the reality of suffering: sometimes we may be persecuted precisely *for* being an active follower of the Way. Early believers then and now in places where faith is a minority understood and understand this kind of suffering well. In this country, we rarely have to deal with pain that comes from expressing or living out our faith. Jesus Christ even suffered at the hands of religious people, who failed to see in him the Messiah and purpose of God. Good people sometimes suffer because of what they believe. Suffering for one's faith can bring about a deeper strength and a greater resolve. As Ernest Hemingway declares in *A Farewell to Arms*, "Somewhere along the way life had broken us all . . . and we were all stronger at the broken places."

Myth #16: Love Is Surging Passion

One of the prevailing contributions of our society's entertainment subculture is the misperception that momentary passion and love are essentially the same. In an environment where people talk of "falling in love"—and "fall" out of love as mood and temperament shift—Hollywood has done a good job of convincing a lot of people that love is basically identified by surging hormones and flashes of emotion. An element of truth has lately appeared on the screen, as recent conversations between lovers have more often employed the words "I want you" and "I need you" as opposed to "I'm in love with you." But the image primarily portrayed in our entertainment industry is one in which people use the word "love" during the first twenty fours in a relationship and jump in bed to "express their love" at the end of a first date. What they are actually doing is giving vent to their hormonal attraction one to another, without much postponed gratification.

In a society where intimacy is poorly understood, such a myopic view of love should not be surprising. The sad misrepresentation that occurs, however, perpetuates the confusion between "needing" and "loving." A central characteristic of adolescent preoccupation is the self. Appropriate energy and focus during those turbulent years needs to be spent on self-awareness and care. The issue becomes a problem for us when we never graduate from self-absorption, and live our adult lives as if the only important needs to be met are our own. Christopher Lash called such preoccupation our *Culture of Narcissism* and declared that we were dealing with heavy doses of it during the last decade of the twentieth century. Lederer and Jackson spoke of the common misuse of the word "love" in our daily conversations, suggesting that most people who use the word really mean "need" (*The Mirages of Marriage* [New York: W.W. Norton, 1968]).

People who indulge in premature sexual intimacy in young adulthood need to understand two problems they are expressing: (1) The early and quick passionate physical response to another person is mainly self-indulgence, not love. People who engage in such exercises are taking care of their own needs and usually using their partners for their own personal satisfaction. They are not "loving" their partners; they are using them. Sexual urges and impulses have little to do with caring for another person, especially at early stages in a relationship. (2) Most persons who engage in early sexual exercises are trying to meet appropriate intimacy needs by employing physical intimacy to find it, and they rarely discover genuine closeness. True intimacy (the kind God made us to share) is a bonding experience that comes in a shared relationship of trust, mutual care, and responsibility that *precedes* sexual intimacy. The disappointing result is that men and women who know each other quite superficially and engage in sexual intercourse often face an unexpected emptiness and dissatisfaction in the relationship following their physical indulgence.

Love is a developing experience between people and begins with the individual's capacity to transcend one's own needs in favor of responding to another person's needs. Love involves the assumption of responsibility in a relationship and the cultivation of respect for another person. Love develops gradually and includes the decision to include another person in the private and vulnerable dimensions of one's life. Love involves care and risk. Passion and physical attraction add to the expression of love but should not be confused with the totality of love.

Myth #17: If People Really Love Me, They Will Guess What I Need

Ah, for the gift of a crystal ball in relationships. How did we ever reach the conclusion that caring for someone means they have clear insight into our needs? Loving someone does not mean we know what they want. How is it possible to guess what someone else needs or wants when even *they* don't know what they want?

Loving people has little to do with guessing what they need. No doubt, if we love someone, we will probably spend time "studying" them and trying to guess—or figure out—what they most want. But in reality, love offers us no crystal ball for gazing into the mystery of another person's life and guessing that person's wants or needs.

The more appropriate adage we may live by, which is far more useful, is "If I really love someone, I will help them learn what I most need and want, so that they can best respond to my needs." Such an approach places the responsibility of disclosure on us, not our partner or friend. Using God as the primary model for relationships, this approach suggests that loving relationships begin not when people expect others to guess their needs, but when they reveal their own needs and expectations as best they can so that their loved ones can succeed in caring for them. Love means wanting to communicate myself as best as I can to my friend, so that he or she can respond appropriately to the relationship I've offered. That is what God did in creation, explaining from the beginning to all human beings—and to Israel—who God is and what God wants and needs in a relationship. Such disclosures were never offered as requirements, but as invitations in the relationship.

In the marriage counseling that I do, I listen carefully for emotional games partners play in relationships. Emotional games are often punitive, for they "set up" the loved one by not revealing an expectation the other person has—and then punishing the other for not guessing it. One of our favorite emotional games is "guess what I need, and when you find out, it's too late." Emotional games are dishonest because they involve withholding information from a companion and then expecting that person to act as if he or she had that information. Another emotional game is called

"Gotcha!" in which we withhold information in regard to a secret "right" answer or behavior and penalize our partner by declaring any response he or she gives as "wrong." The sad dynamic in both these relational games is that we are expecting our partners to "fail," and we make sure that they do by withholding critical information.

Loving someone actually means working hard to help that person understand us. It means revealing as much of ourselves as possible to a companion so that he or she may love us more intelligently and respond to us in ways that increase our bonding. Loving as an adult means letting go of childish ways, as Paul said in 1 Corinthians 13:11, so that we are no longer seeking someone to "parent" us, but someone with whom to share a mutually responsible partnership.

Myth #18: I Cannot Make It without the Support/Love of (Name)

Our inclination to believe that we are dependent upon others for our survival is strong. Children have the right to this belief because it is accurate for dependent human beings on the road to adulthood. But adults don't "require" any certain relationship to survive. How many popular "love songs" carry the message "I cannot live without you"? We have been conditioned by society to believe we cannot function—or live—without the love or approval of certain people. The reality is that we can live without the love, blessing, or approval of anyone, even though we'd like to have it. We've learned to tell ourselves we couldn't make it without the support of a certain person, but that isn't so. Sandra Eng, describing the challenging childhoods of several successful adults, celebrated their capacity for survival and endurance in a book titled *The Resilient Adult*. The truth about us is that God has equipped us to overcome many adversities on the journey to adulthood, including the loss of parents, the abandonment of supportive family, debilitating illnesses, abusive relationships, horrendous crises, and the betrayal of trusted significant others.

We are capable of overcoming many obstacles, and we can survive the loss of a crucial relationship. What we usually struggle with when we say "we can't make it" without a certain relationship is that we don't want to make it without that relationship or don't like it that we have lost that particular relationship. We wish we had control over people's responses to us, and we do not like it when they don't respond as we wish they would. But that says little about our capacity for survival or success without them. No doubt we will grieve the significant loss experienced by someone's withdrawal of friendship, care, or love. Grief over the loss of a relationship upon which we have conferred significant importance is a major bereavement. The loss will occasion a journey of deep grief and we will probably require months, or more than a year, to regain stability and joy. But we *can* get over it, and we shall if we allow ourselves to move on.

Our greatest challenge in healing is our temptation to try to control another person's response to us—as if we could (see myth #19, "If I work hard at it, I can control other people"). Other people don't have power over us unless we give them that power. To overcome our fear that any relationship has control over us, we should take the time to examine what we are saying to ourselves about the relationship and loss. If we tell ourselves repeatedly that

we cannot function without a given person, we will convince ourselves of it, even though it is false. Once we take note of our
"invented reality," we can challenge it by declaring it to be the
untruth that it is, and we can resist repeating the myth to ourselves
as a created mantra.

We may then care for ourselves by not requiring that we dis-
miss our loss as if we had no deep feelings for our connection and
by giving ourselves time to heal from the loss. The depth of the
relationship lost will determine the length and intensity of our
grief. Time and care will lead us beyond survival to function ade-
quately, then well, and to begin to hope again. But to tell ourselves
that we cannot live without the love or blessing of another person
is a lie.

Myth #19: If I Work Hard at It, I Can Control Other People

What an attractive fiction! Many of us spend an entire lifetime
either believing that we can control others or trying to do so. No
doubt it is possible to set controls over other people's behaviors—
temporarily. But the myth we are challenging here is the notion
that we can control other people's thoughts and actions without
their consent. I have no control over someone else's thoughts. I
have no control over anyone's behavior. The only control we have
over someone else's thoughts, attitudes, or actions is *if they give us
that control.* The fact is that we often surrender control of our
thoughts or actions to someone else by allowing them to have an
influence over what we think or do. No one can control our

thoughts but us—unless we offer them the power to do so. No one can control our actions unless we give them the power to do so.

Nor do we have power over someone else's thoughts or actions without their permission. Made in the image of God, each of us has control and power over our own thoughts and actions. We may surrender our control over either of these personal gifts at any time. Children often are influenced (appropriately) in thought and action by their parents, but they choose to accept that control. We adults regularly surrender power over our thoughts and behaviors for a variety of similar reasons. Some of the common reasons for surrendering control of our thoughts and actions are fear, ignorance, and love. We may choose to think or act as someone else tells us to because we are afraid of the consequences for disobeying them. We may choose to behave or think as someone else suggests out of ignorance that we have the power to do as we please. And we may choose to think or act in a particular way to please someone else because we love them and want to do what they want us to do.

Try as we might, however, we have no power in ourselves to control another person's thoughts or behaviors *without their giving us that power*. I may wish that I could make someone else love me, and I may act in particular ways to persuade that someone else to care for me. But whatever thoughts or feelings they have in response to my persuasion are theirs in origin, not mine. *They* are in control of their thoughts, feelings, and responses to me. The most I can do in any relationship is to ask for particular responses or invite specific reactions; the other person has the power and the control to decide how he or she will, in fact, respond. No one has unusual powers over anyone else, unless that other person has granted such power.

God has always made the same assumptions in relationships with us. God never forces a response in a relationship. God always invites, pleads, asks. God does not try to control our responses— or they would not be ours, and free. They would be reactions controlled by God, and therefore not voluntary but coerced. The very character of God is at work also in us, in that we human beings only respond voluntarily when we are given the freedom to respond—or not. Any attempt to control or manipulate another person's thoughts or actions is a coercive gesture at odds with God's principle of individual respect and personal choice. Healthy human relationships function best on the basis of this same premise. We cannot control someone else's thoughts or behaviors anyway; but to try to do so is to violate the fabric of individual personhood. As tempting as it appears, any attempt to control someone else's thoughts, feelings, or actions ignores the sacred gift of individuality bestowed upon us by God.

Section 3

Affirmations That Enrich a Journey to Adulthood

There are some foundational truths that shape our belief about the world we live in and the journey toward adulthood. Here are several important principles we affirm that shape our travel:

(1) *We are made in the image of God.* This presupposition has to do with who we are and who made us. We believe that we were made by a loving and purposeful God and made in the image (character and demeanor) of that Creator. We were created with purposes, goals, and abilities by one who designed us to become human reflections of the Maker. We are, therefore, persons with rich and meaningful destinies. We were each designed by a Master Designer.

(2) *We are responsible for our own thoughts, choices, and actions.* As reflectors of the Creator, we have been made capable of creating our own thoughts and behaviors. We have been given the privilege of creating our own destinies, journeys, and goals. We are also, therefore, responsible for our own thoughts and actions and every choice we make. We are not puppets who must follow someone else's direction or thought; we have free will—and free choices and actions—within the range of human limitations.

(3) *We are placed in families to learn how to choose, live, love, think, and act for ourselves.* In an atmosphere of love, grace, and encouragement, we were each intended a cluster of mature adults who were devoted enough to us to model the image of God in a human form, so that one day we would also become a unique, mature human being. We are not solitary human beings created to learn all by ourselves. We were all meant to have been given loving "coaches" who mentor and model the qualities and hopes that God designed and wished for us.

(4) *God wants to work with us to bring to fruition our many abilities and vocational seeds.* The Creator who designed us wants to play an active part in our lives to encourage, produce, and direct our many capabilities. This is contingent upon the degree to which we invite God to participate in our development. God wants to be companion to us in all the seasons of our lives. God does not force himself or his purposes upon anyone, but is eager to respond to our invitation to participate in our lives and development. The Maker of life wants to partner with us in the development of our own stories but does not want to force that invitation on us. We are invited by God to cooperate with the purposes and goals the Maker designed when making us.

(5) *We are capable of gaining and growing in every experience of life.* Grace is the God-given gift whereby every choice and behavior we exercise is an opportunity for good—even if a mistake or poor choice. Any of our destructive behaviors or choices can be redeemed for good. God offers us the invitation to try several avenues and detours in life and makes it possible for us to profit even from our failures, poor choices, and harmful behaviors. God can make good from any bad choice.

(6) *Faith can gain strength in the face of the unknown.* Mystery and lack of clarity can act as allies to faith rather than enemies to our journey of belief. Faith is stretched and tested by the unknown so that the future and any darkness ahead are opportunities for the development of personal belief. Mystery and darkness are not our enemies on the journey; venturing into the dark is itself an act of faith and hope.

(7) *Faith in ourselves is an unpredictable experience that ebbs and flows.* Our confidence and belief in ourselves often fades and sometimes surges during our lifetime. Neither of these fragile movements has much to do with our faith in *God*; rather, they are mostly signs of our struggle to believe in ourselves. Doubting ourselves and our capacities is a normal and recurring experience during the pilgrimage to adulthood. Our doubts are not a measure of our hope or faith.

(8) *God is present and involved with us even in the silent seasons of life.* There are moments and seasons on the life journey in which silence and stillness are active ingredients in the process of our personal growth. Like the work of winter, seeds fallow in the preparatory stages of darkness and quiet to emerge in spring. Silence should not be interpreted as the absence or punishment of

God. In quietness and darkness, God does significant preparatory work!

(9) *The community of faith was created for companionship as we discover and grow.* We are pilgrims together on a journey of discovery and personal development, and the church was designed to offer nurture and community for us as we experiment and grow. We are not lone pilgrims on a solitary journey. We are meant to travel through life in companionship and in communion with others.

(10) *Our promises and commitments to persons, causes, and actions define our character and reflect the nature of God.* Making and keeping promises is essential to personal growth and responsible identity. Promises and commitments are neither unnecessary luxuries nor trivial matters; they are indispensable to our personal development and maturity as "reflectors" of God's character. Making promises defines who we are and who we commit ourselves to become.

(11) *Suffering and struggle are normal ingredients in the development of purpose, focus, and identity.* No worthwhile growth or self-development happens without struggle and pain. Suffering contributes character and depth to belief and commitment. Comfort and pain avoidance are not primary goals in the movement toward self-fulfillment and growth.

(12) *Personal development takes time and patience.* Some of the most important experiences and choices in life only develop with the expenditure of time, effort, and patience. Endurance and determination are attributes that breed maturity. Instant gratification and immediate results have little to do with faith and even less to do with enduring satisfaction. Maturity takes time to develop.

(13) *Risk and vulnerability are crucial to personal fulfillment.* Personal investment and care cannot engage vocation, cause, and people without openness, trust, and the willingness to be hurt. We cannot love "safely" or care from a distance. Vulnerability feeds love, and its absence breeds a disconnection and disaffection from human and divine community

(14) *God provides a greater abundance of opportunities and choices in life than we can ever exhaust.* We are each designed to experience many vocations, causes, and purposes. We will never exhaust the gifts and talents with which God has equipped us. There is more to discover, develop, and do than we will ever cover in a lifetime. God has gifted us with more skills than we can ever fully employ.

Section 4

How Will
We Know
When We've
Grown Up?

When I was a child, I spoke like a child, I thought like a child, I reasoned like a child; when I became an adult, I put an end to childish ways.

(1 Cor 13:11)

We have identified ways to tell when a human being has physically become an adult. We ask how old they are and look for visual signs: height, muscular development, and general appearance. What are some of the signs that an individual has reached emotional and spiritual adulthood? Several clues help us identify an emotionally mature adult. Perhaps we can also point out several distinct characteristics that confirm *spiritual* adulthood.

When do we know that a person has reached emotional maturity? Here are a few important questions whose answers give us evidence of emotional maturity:

Do I Know that I'm Not the Only One Who Matters?

Some young people focus on themselves so long that they fail to learn that other people and their needs also matter. I "graduate" into adulthood when I grasp the insight that I am a creature living in community—not all by myself. Self-preoccupation is a priority in adolescence when we are learning about our identity and individuality. But we were never intended to live as if no one else mattered; God placed us in families to understand that we are part of a community and that we affect that community and are affected by it. The choices we make as adults include a consideration of others. The famous John Donne adage, "no man is an island, entire of itself" (John Donne, *Devotions Upon Emergent Occasions*, Meditation XVII) reaffirms the biblical truth that we were meant to think and act as persons who are part of a community. To exist is to interact with others and to connect with them.

I do not live my life in a vacuum. The choices I make affect the people with whom I am connected. When I learn that my voice is mine, but that I belong to a human choir of voices, then I begin to understand the basic nature of creation and the created order. I am related to a family and to a community of people.

Am I Capable of Postponing Immediate Gratification?

As infants we enter the world with a tendency to require immediate response to our felt needs. Hunger and discomfort are primary concerns, followed quickly by the need for sleep and safety. We learn early how to make demands for immediate gratification and often spend the first years of life learning to adjust to the reality that all our needs will not be met upon request. Postponing the satisfaction of our demands is a rude awakening to a world that will not always please us or respond to our needs at our beckoning.

Children and teenagers often arrive at late adolescence without ever having grasped the reality of postponed gratification. Some so-called adults move through young adulthood—or through life—without ever having learned how to postpone the satisfaction of their needs or whims. One of the significant issues in growing up is learning that we must postpone the meeting of some of our needs in order to meet other, more immediately pressing needs. We also grow up when we begin to accept the fact that sometimes the meeting of our needs may be set aside in order to meet someone else's needs first. Such an insight is a necessary precondition for a mature friendship, a marriage, and the care of children we choose to parent.

There are several aspects of this characteristic that affect our capacity to love. When we place someone else's needs before our own, we are expressing significant care for them. We demonstrate thoughtfulness and self-control when we set aside the tending to our own concerns in favor of responding to the concern of another person. In essence, we cease being self-focused, or self-centered, when we demonstrate a capacity to place someone else's needs ahead of our own.

Such development mirrors the image of God, who defines care and love by creating human beings and spending time and energy in the pursuit of their needs. The capacity to postpone meeting our own needs first is crucial to the role of servanthood. To serve someone else entails the willingness to subjugate my own desires and needs in an effort to offer care to another person.

Do I Assume Responsibility for My Own Behavior?

Somewhere along the maturation process we discontinue the practice of believing someone else is responsible for our actions or choices. As important as parents are in shaping some of our behaviors and habits, they cannot be made responsible for choices and behaviors we exhibit as full-grown adults. Apart from congenital issues and serious emotional limitations, we adults "grow up" when we take responsibility for our own actions, choices, and attitudes. As persons with the capacity to think, feel, and act on our own, we are also persons who can assume responsibility for who we are and what we do.

We consider someone an emotionally mature person when he exhibits signs that he has begun to take charge of his life for himself. An emotionally responsible person believes he is in charge of his own thoughts and that no one can control his thoughts but himself. He also assumes responsibility for the choices he makes in life, so that he is no longer holding anyone else accountable for his selections. Likewise, the emotionally focused adult is in charge of his own actions and understands that he—and no one else—has control over his actions.

The responsible adult also knows that spiritually she is the only person accountable for her thoughts, actions, and choices. Her faith is grounded on his own convictions, not the borrowed beliefs of a parent or spiritual guardian. She does not blame others for her behaviors ("the devil made me do it") but takes full responsibility for her life and its direction.

Am I Capable of Loving Someone Else?

Such a question might seem unnecessary, since we may assume that every human being is capable of loving. The challenge, however, is to make a distinction between "needing" and "loving." We can choose to relate to a variety of persons for the purpose of meeting our own needs. We may suggest that we care about someone else on the basis of what they *mean* to us, but quite often what we mean by saying we "care" for someone is that we appreciate his or her attention to our needs.

Adolescents are appropriately self-absorbed, since the focus of their development is on self-identity and self-differentiation. Youth often "care" for someone only to the extent that those persons provide them a benefit in return for interest shown. One of the critical transitions from late adolescence to young adulthood is when we begin to demonstrate a capacity to focus on another person instead of ourselves and to be concerned about their welfare. People who learn to become interested in another person for the sake of that person have grown up in their understanding of relationships. They have found ways to avoid being self-centered. They have learned to care for others.

Such a shift in self-understanding is essential for both genuine friendship and marriage. Friendship requires a mutuality of concern in which two people engage in the care of one another in a balanced relationship; both participants offer value and show interest in the other person. The marriage partnership is healthiest when two persons have learned to value each other and work for the welfare of their partner.

Erik Erikson identified "care" as a central developmental issue in the adult life journey and declared that the most prevailing signal of such an adult stage was the capacity to nurture and sustain one's own children, while also providing for the increased limitations of one's aging parents. Young adulthood is a rehearsal of such strengths, as individuals firm up their potential for fidelity, identity, and intimacy by understanding who they are, what boundaries exist between themselves and others, and how to value and respond to others for their own sake. I am capable of loving if I can place someone else's life and concerns ahead of mine. If I can do that, I'm showing signs of emotional and spiritual maturity.

Am I Willing to Pay the Price for the Choices I Make?

One of the characteristic struggles of growing up is deciding whether or not we stand behind the choices we make. A challenge most parents experience is that of teaching their offspring that every decision they make has a price to be paid—and that each person is responsible to "pay the price" for the choices and options he or she exercises. A swimmer my wife has taught has chosen to try out for the national Olympic team; she gets up early every weekday, arrives at the school swimming pool by 6:30 A.M., and swims for an hour and a half. When many of her friends relax and play after school, she returns to the gym for two more hours of steady practice and exercise. Like other disciplined young people, she has decided that hours of practice weekly are her price to reach her chosen goal.

A young man down the street decided that he was going to join a respected law firm and become a partner in the system within ten years. He clerked long hours, studied cases into the night, and accepted all assignments he was offered. Single and never married at the age of thirty-seven, he often talks about his isolation and loneliness. He takes no time for recreation or relaxation and feels "on the margin" at church, mainly because he attends infrequently and knows hardly anyone in the fellowship. He's struggling with an emptiness he feels in his life but believes he is close to becoming a senior partner in the firm and is afraid of slowing down. He apparently has accepted the price he has paid to achieve a primary goal in his career.

We make choices all the time. By the time we are of age, a sure sign of emotional maturity is our willingness to accept responsibility for our own choices and to assume the consequences for decisions and options we exercise.

Do I Understand and Respect Boundaries in My Relationships?

Some people grow up in families that set and teach extreme boundaries: they either require family members to have no sense of a separate self and therefore no separate identity (fused family relationships), or they distance themselves so much from family members that they are not connected to each other emotionally. When we grow up in such family systems, we have to struggle to find our own individual balance between closeness and distance from others. Growing up emotionally and spiritually in such cir-cumstances means negotiating a personal sense of oneself apart from the family we grew up in so that we set our own boundaries as adults in our relationships.

An emotionally healthy individual is one who has learned to recognize and respect the boundaries other people set in relation-ships without having to adopt those boundaries as his or her own. An adult can choose how much closeness and distance she wants in different relationships and exercise those choices individually in dealing with different people. If I can relate to family members on the basis of my own chosen boundaries, I have achieved a measure of maturity that reflects adulthood. Such a choice allows other people to determine where to set the boundaries in a relationship with me but still allows me to decide under what boundaries I shall choose to operate.

An emotionally mature adult can decide how much contact and closeness she wants from a friend or a family member on the basis of her own needs. If the family or friend does not respond to (or respect) that choice, then a mature adult can decide what options to take for himself. I may choose to distance myself from a family member who does not respect my boundaries as an indi-vidual, to protect myself appropriately from invasion, control, or manipulation by that person. I may decide to spend energy engag-ing in more closeness to a friend who struggles with intimacy. In either case, the other person may choose to accept, reject, or counter the choices and boundaries I offer, but an adult emotion-ally is conscious of and intentional about the boundaries he or she sets.

Do I Have My Own Voice?

Earlier we've mentioned Gordon Allport's reference to "second-hand" and "firsthand fittings." Every child and young person stores away beliefs, attitudes, opinions, and behaviors their parents and significant others have taught them through the years. Each person experiences a gradual (or sudden) transition in life when she begins to "own" or discard this collection of borrowed messages and actions. A youth becomes an adult when he "comes to himself," to use Luke's phrase about the prodigal. To do so means to see oneself in a new light, ceasing to behave out of reaction to others or selective inattention to self, and to begin to choose and incorporate a set of guidelines and actions that is internalized and claimed personally.

A wise director of a clinical pastoral education program I took suggested that an individual only experienced adulthood when financially independent of parents. The strings attached to any financial dependence make self-identity a fuzzy reality at best, and the one in three chronological adults in this country who currently live under the roof of their family of origin can attest to that dynamic. Somehow any signs that suggest a form of dependence render each of us less than our full selves.

That is why the young person who returns to live with parents after college, the military, a divorce, or a personal setback enters an awkward and often difficult environment. People who gain some independence and then relinquish it have trouble reversing their courses. Young adults and parents alike struggle to adjust to such changes that, though often temporary, create an imbalance and new learning curve for every member of the affected family. Parents' temptation to protect children from emotional and financial duress may work against some of the most important lessons young people might learn about growing up and about having and hearing their own voices as they make life-altering decisions.

There is also an added energy that comes from "owning" our own choices and defining ourselves. When we assume responsibility for our beliefs and choices, we gain confidence in ourselves and discover an internal strength that comes from affirming our own separate identity. When I "stand on my own two feet," I gain new power—the power that comes from declaring myself a person in my own right, with thoughts, attitudes, and actions that are mine, not someone else's.

Am I Capable of Distinguishing between Making Mistakes and Being a Failure?

Another way of talking about this issue is to ask whether I've learned to make a distinction between failing at something and being a failure. Psychologists often describe this thought process as "universalizing": we conclude on the basis of one or two failed actions or choices that *we* are failures! Simply put, we generalize from a few experiences to "all," and erroneously decide that everything we try is a failure. Elijah employs such generalizing in 1 Kings 19, when he concludes from one traumatic experience (Jezebel's attack on Israelite prophets) that all is lost and runs, with suicidal thoughts, to hide in a cave and perhaps die. The "prodigal son" betrays the same excessive overgeneralization: he concludes on the basis of his recent behavior that he is "no longer worthy to be called" the father's son, seeing himself as a total failure (Luke 15:21). Maturity entails finding perspective in life. By design, late adolescence and young adulthood are periods in our lives when we are called to experiment and examine different preferences and possibilities. There is no better way to determine if a certain kind of work, choice, or action fits us than to try it out. In such an environment, we also need the freedom to discontinue what we try and to fail in our trying, without a verdict of self-worthlessness or complete failure. Extreme responses to any issues in life are the stuff of adolescence. I show signs of maturity when I can take my mistakes seriously without being overwhelmed or paralyzed by them. Even one of the thieves crucified next to Jesus achieved enough perspective to ask the Son of God, "Lord, remember me when you come into your kingdom" (Luke 23:42).

Do I Demonstrate Adequate Self-control over My Emotions and Actions?

Children and adolescents often respond with a tantrum when they don't get their way. Some people express their anger and frustration in destructive or violent ways. A key component of emotional maturity is a demonstrated capacity to exercise some degree of control over deeply felt emotions. Developing and practicing such controls is a function of maturation that can only be accomplished over a period of time. An emotionally mature adult does not resort to inappropriate or irresponsible behaviors when dealing with an issue over which he differs with someone else. If anyone can elicit enough anger or frustration in me that I lose control over my actions or responses, I am confessing that I haven't learned how to "bridle" myself enough to cause no harm and that I actually allow other people to have control over my thoughts and actions.

Abusive actions or responses are a sure sign of immaturity. People who have not learned to control their tempers or cannot place boundaries on their reactions to others haven't grown up emotionally and spiritually. Each of us has known adults who have grown up physically but show little control over their emotions. The often applauded Samson is a dark example of someone who was physically an adult but emotionally and spiritually a petulant child. His story (Judg 14–16) is punctuated with impetuous and irresponsible decisions, culminating in his own death while seeking revenge over the Philistines who had blinded him. His final self-destructive act—like the prayer that preceded it—is more a public display of his anger and self-centeredness than an exercise in faith.

Personnel experts across the vocational spectrum testify that the majority of terminations in most workplaces are a result of poor relational behaviors and much less a product of skill limitations. If I want to be considered an adult by my peers and superiors, I had better learn to exercise control over my emotions and my actions.

Are My Faith Values My Own?

Adolescents move into early adulthood with a number of untested and borrowed beliefs. Unless we have faced a major crisis that forces us to examine and evaluate what we believe, we often operate on one of two fronts: (1) we give superficial (verbal) assent to values and beliefs others have taught us, rarely testing their veracity, or (2) we react to the "secondhand" convictions of significant others and choose to live by an opposite or distinct code of faith statements. The first option usually leads to a series of reflections and habits that are less than meaningful and cannot last long in an adult and complex world (notice the children of Israel in captivity and unable to "sing the songs of Zion in a foreign land" [Ps 137]). The second option delivers an equally unpleasant set of affirmations, for those who believe in anything by *reaction* to something else are also not free to affirm anything much for themselves.

The third possibility for faith seekers is for us to do our homework and come up with a faith we can affirm and own as ours. Whether exploring what we have been handed down in order to see if it fits us "for the long haul" or carefully choosing to affirm convictions for ourselves without having to do so by reacting to what we've been given, each of us arrives at adulthood "spiritually" by embracing a tested personal faith. A childhood faith must grow into an adult spiritual experience, or I have not "put an end to childish ways" (1 Cor 13:11, RSV).

Have I Learned to Live with Ambivalence?

Psychologists call "ambivalence" the coexistence of opposing forces or issues. Children grow up in a simplistic world where they see choices as clearly distinct as black from white. The adolescent world introduces choices and options that often blur the clear distinction between such realities. By the time an individual has reached adulthood, he or she should have come to terms with the presence of "gray" issues and choices that are complex and that do not lend themselves to clear or simplistic options. There are realities that require a position somewhere in between the boundaries of black and white. The mother in Sudan struggles with ambivalence when she chooses to feed one of her children well so that he will survive, and in the process chooses not to feed her other three children, knowing that if she feeds them all, she will feed them inadequately, and they will all eventually die. The reservist in the National Guard who chooses to stay home with his family and children rather than return to Iraq faces the ostracism of his friends and coworkers for his choice. The plant manager of twenty-six years must choose whether to follow the unethical new policies he has just been handed or resign and lose his benefits and pensions. The patriarch who wants to be faithful to God is given the choice of obeying his Creator or sparing his son's life (Abraham and Isaac).

William Barclay identified the same issue in a lecture I attended years ago in Scotland. He said to us, referring to the parable of the Great Feast in Luke 14:15-24: "The trouble with our choices in life is not so much in choosing between good and evil things, or right and wrong; our struggle comes in deciding how to choose among the many good things, what is best, and among several evil choices, what is worst." Life is not always clear or simple. Maturity involves dealing with life as it often confronts us: complex, difficult, gray, with choices that sometimes require a mixture of contradictory values.

I show the maturity of an adult when I realize that more money may bring more pleasure but may also take a toll on my health or time with family. As Christians, we are regularly faced with alternatives that hold good options for us but may also exact a heavy price. Growing up means coming to terms with choices that offer mixed blessings and limited good. I still remember the agony of a congressman friend of mine who first faced a legislative bill that would greatly reduce the poverty of a group of Native Americans in his state, but that had attached to it a major provision for the establishment of casinos and gambling houses in the same area. Have I learned to live with a sizable amount of ambivalence in life?

Do I See Life as a Gift or as an Entitlement?

The difference between these two outlooks colors my response to daily experiences. Many of us have grown up in a country where we have celebrated our "rights" as individuals. We probably have more freedom in the United States than most people experience in other places. Unfortunately, children and young people of such an environment often confuse these significant freedoms with a right to do whatever they wish. Most of us would quickly affirm that our freedoms have limitations and that those limits begin where another person's boundaries and rights begin. We generally understand that our freedom is not to do as we please regardless of anyone else's life or rights, but to follow a common set of rules that respect the rights and privileges of other people. We live in a community in which other people share our rights.

Christians, however, live by an additional assumption. Followers of Christ are not only preoccupied with their rights and entitled privileges; they are governed by the assumption that life is a *gift* from God, not a privilege anyone has earned. Accordingly, as a believer, I am not consumed with or controlled by my rights, but seeking to follow the purposes and opportunities this gift of life has provided me. I am not "entitled" to life; it was given to me by an act of grace—the grace of a loving God who chose to offer me an opportunity to live, to create, to choose, to love, etc. When I begin to understand that every day is a gift provided by the one who made me, I see and receive life in a qualitatively different way. I am not entitled to life or freedom; the only rights I have come from the God who made me. Life is a privilege only in the sense that God has made me and shares this outstanding gift daily with me and others.

Can a Cause I Embrace Be Challenged without My Feeling Personally Rejected?

One of the most significant insights in the development of a mature adult perspective is our discovery that a particular point of view we hold can be challenged without affecting our self-worth. Our capacity to separate our issues from our selfhood is essential to personal growth. Peter was severely admonished by Jesus for his naive point of view on Christ's mission (Matt 16:21-23), but he did not conclude from Christ's comments that he had been personally rejected as a follower. When I can offer an opinion or advocate a cause without concluding that I've been attacked or rejected when it is challenged, I've "grown up" emotionally and spiritually.

Students of logic identify this capacity to challenge someone's point of view without attacking the person who holds it. In debates and arguments, the Latin designation of a personal verbal attack is *argumentum ad hominem.* The phrase refers to a speaker's attempt to attack the *person* presenting an issue rather than discussing the issue itself. People display an "adult" or grownup perspective when they evidence a capacity to distinguish between an issue being presented and the person who presented it. There is no need to take offense at the challenge of an argument. While I may differ with someone's point of view, I have achieved emotional adulthood when I can allow the individual to express a different point of view without rejecting him or her as a person.

This distinction should work to my benefit as well when evaluating my own thoughts and opinions. As an adult, I should be able to entertain a thought without being so connected to it emotionally that a rejection of it is a personal indictment on me as a person. Thoughts are mental exercises, creations of my own—not my whole selfhood. They do not contain my entire worth. As fragile as any of us can feel about whether our opinions or thoughts are taken seriously, I hope we can each eventually learn that any point of view we offer is not the whole measure of our contribution, intelligence, capacity—or acceptance.

When I can separate myself enough from the thoughts and opinions I share to allow them scrutiny, I have achieved a level of self-understanding that hints strongly of emotional and spiritual maturity.

Conclusion

We live in a complex world where growing up is not easy to do. Adult attitudes and behaviors take time to develop and don't automatically appear at chronological maturity. The communities of family and congregation can provide significant guidance and modeling for individual personal development, and every adolescent has a major contribution to make in his or her journey toward adulthood.

One more set of suggestions follows about how the local church can assist in this challenging and rewarding journey from late adolescence to mature adulthood:

(1) Create an atmosphere where children and adolescents can regularly learn that God has placed many talents within them and in their vocational paths. Remind each child that our biblical models for vocation reflect both multiple vocations and sequential vocations. Many of our biblical heroes followed several vocations one after another, and many of them possessed talents for several callings and skills (Exod 3:1).

(2) Help children and youth understand that God's call often follows a process of several "conversations," so that following God's will involves a patient process of discovery, development, and maturation. A call mostly evolves and grows with time and exploration. (See 1 Sam 3:19.)

(3) Help adolescents understand the value and the process of making their belief systems their own along the way. Otherwise, they travel into adulthood with borrowed beliefs, which rarely pass

the testing of valleys and challenges on the vocational journey. (See Gen 28:16.)

(4) Assist youth to struggle with and wrestle with their doubts and questions so that they learn to take them seriously and have an opportunity to emerge in adulthood with a stronger personal faith. Encourage questions and inquisitiveness as avenues to stretching the fabric of human faith. (See John 2:4.)

(5) Interpret the experience of personal "timeouts" on the journey of development so that young people may use "fallow" and winter seasons as opportunities to marinate their faith and vocation during silent and slow periods in their personal growth. Sometimes the readiness to apprehend, discover, grow, and explore is not present, and we must wait for it. Teachable moments only occur when time, personal development, and openness converge. (See Luke 2:51-52.)

(6) Teach children and adolescents (and young adults!) that there are prices to be paid for each goal and choice made in life, and that sacrifice for a worthy cause is essential to biblical growth. Help them understand that there are few "immediate rewards" in Christian discipleship and that some of their most valuable purposes will only be achieved through pain, postponement, and suffering. (See Deut 34:4.)

(7) Teach and model to youth and children that life is not about controlling other people but about inspiring them and loving them. Give them a wider view of power than society's lie that manipulation, money, and self-indulgence are the primary forces to acquire. (See Luke 19:8.)

(8) Develop in children and youth an appreciation and capacity for solitude and privacy. Bless each person's need for creative boundaries that allow for privacy, self-reflection, and personal

definition. Encourage exercises that engage the inner resources of a person's soul. Help young people develop the gift of solitude and creative self-expression by trying different ways to read, pray, reflect, and create. (See Mark 6:46.)

(9) Teach children the value of doing for others, helping others, and meeting someone else's needs before their own. Show them the pleasure of giving from a generous heart. (See Mark 12:43-44.)

(10) Encourage respect for another person's point of view so that they learn to distinguish between differing with a person and still valuing him as another person made in God's image. Show them how to preserve the dignity of another person while differing with her point of view. (See 2 Kgs 5:2-3.)

(11) Challenge each child and youth to identify some of their prejudices and stereotypes, and help them discover ways to examine the premature judgments they make about an issue or a person. (See Acts 10:47.)

(12) Help children and young people learn the importance of taking responsibility for their actions, beliefs, and choices. A critical step in personal maturity arises when a person assumes responsibility for himself and takes ownership of what he does and says. (See 2 Sam 12:1-7.)

The Maker of life joins family and church in the exciting developmental journey toward adulthood and maturity, offering deep fulfillment and satisfaction to all who risk the adventure. May the issues we've offered here provide helpful "signposts" on the road to our full development as believers.

Brave journey—and may God provide!